Greek Mythology Book For Teens

CRAFTED BY SKRIUWER

At **Skriuwer**, we're more than just a team—we're a global community of people who love books. In Frisian, "Skriuwer" means "writer," and that's at the heart of what we do: creating and sharing books with readers worldwide. Wherever you are in the world, **Skriuwer** is here to inspire learning.

Frisian is one of the oldest languages in Europe, closely related to English and Dutch, and is spoken by about **500,000 people** in the province of **Friesland** (Fryslân), located in the northern Netherlands. It's the second official language of the Netherlands, but like many minority languages, Frisian faces the challenge of survival in a modern, globalized world.

We're using the money we earn to promote the Frisian language.

For more information, contact : **kontakt@skriuwer.com** (www.skriuwer.com)

Disclaimer:
The images in this book are creative reinterpretations of historical scenes. While every effort was made to accurately capture the essence of the periods depicted, some illustrations may include artistic embellishments or approximations. They are intended to evoke the atmosphere and spirit of the times rather than serve as precise historical records.

TABLE OF CONTENTS

CHAPTER 6: MORTALS AND THE GODS

- *Worship, sacrifice, and humility*
- *Hubris leading to divine punishment*
- *Mortals achieving greatness through godly favor*

CHAPTER 7: HEROES IN GREEK MYTHOLOGY

- *Semi-divine ancestry and heroic traits*
- *The heroic cycle of quests and trials*
- *Flaws and moral lessons they embody*

CHAPTER 8: THE TROJAN WAR

- *Paris's judgment and Helen's abduction*
- *Greek forces and Troy's mighty walls*
- *The Trojan Horse and consequences of war*

CHAPTER 9: ODYSSEUS AND HIS JOURNEY

- *Cunning hero's prolonged return from Troy*
- *Encounters with monsters and enchantresses*
- *Triumph at home through wit and perseverance*

CHAPTER 10: PERSEUS AND THE GORGONS

- *Prophecy forcing a perilous quest*
- *Divine gifts enabling Medusa's defeat*
- *Rescuing Andromeda and fulfilling destiny*

CHAPTER 11: THESEUS AND THE MINOTAUR

- Athens under tribute to Crete
- Ariadne's thread guiding the labyrinth
- Tragedy from a broken promise to King Aegeus

CHAPTER 12: HERCULES AND HIS TWELVE LABORS

- Origins steeped in Hera's wrath
- Impossible tasks proving strength and cunning
- Final redemption and ascent to Olympus

CHAPTER 13: JASON AND THE ARGONAUTS

- Gathering legendary heroes on the Argo
- Medea's magic aiding the quest
- Tragic end of Jason's ambitions

CHAPTER 14: THE UNDERWORLD

- Hades's domain and its rivers
- Regions for ordinary souls, heroes, and sinners
- Daring journeys by Orpheus, Theseus, and Hercules

CHAPTER 15: STRANGE CREATURES

- Centaurs, Cyclopes, and hybrid beasts
- Monstrous threats testing heroism
- Moral allegories of chaos vs. order

CHAPTER 1

The Land and People of Ancient Greece

1.1 Overview of the Ancient Greek Landscape

Ancient Greece was not a single country in the way we might picture a modern nation. Instead, it was a collection of lands spread out across rocky mountains, rolling hills, and scattered islands in the sea. These separate lands were home to different groups of people, each with their own customs and ways of life. Yet, they also shared a common language and some common beliefs. Over time, they came to see themselves as Greeks, even though they lived in different areas.

The land of ancient Greece is often described as rugged and uneven. There are steep mountains that cut the mainland into smaller sections. Valleys lie between these mountains, and they offered places for crops to grow and animals to graze. But there was not a lot of flat farmland, so people looked to the sea for survival. Fishing and trading by boat became very important. The Greeks became skilled sailors, making their way across the Mediterranean Sea and beyond. They carried goods like olive oil and pottery to foreign ports and brought back metals, grains, and other resources.

Many Greek communities were built around natural harbors on the coast. The salt air from the sea was a part of everyday life. Island communities, in particular, depended on fishing, local trades, and the occasional farmland tucked between rocky hills. Some islands were known for special types of stone or metal that were valuable for trade. These different resources helped shape each region's character.

Because of the rugged land, Greek communities stayed mostly separate from each other. Instead of being one large kingdom under a single ruler, groups formed **city-states**, called **poleis** (singular: **polis**). Each city-state had its own government and its own way of life. They might share religious festivals or form alliances, but they often had differences in laws or customs. The mountains acted like natural barriers, making travel by land tough. Still, the shared language and stories kept them connected in spirit.

1.2 Early Settlements and Growth of City-States

Historians believe that people began to settle in what we now call Greece many thousands of years ago. Over time, these early settlers created small communities that depended on farming, herding, and fishing. The people built simple homes and lived close to their animals. They slowly learned how to cultivate crops like barley, wheat, and olives. Olives became important because they could be used for oil, which was a key product for lighting, cooking, and trade.

As centuries passed, some communities grew larger. They built walls for protection and developed local leadership. Within these communities, people gathered in central meeting areas, which later became known as the **agora**. The agora was a public space used for markets, gatherings, and debates about civic matters. In time, each community formed its own system of government. Some had kings or chiefs, while others moved toward more communal systems where citizens had a say in decisions.

Because travel by land was tough, city-states often interacted through sea routes. They traded goods such as wine, olive oil, and pottery for metals and grains from other regions. Trade made some city-states wealthy, and that wealth sometimes led to rivalry. City-states would compete not only in terms of power, but also in sporting events and cultural achievements. This spirit of rivalry pushed them to excel in art, architecture, and literature.

Some well-known city-states, like Athens and Sparta, had unique identities. Athens valued learning, art, and new ideas. Sparta focused on military training and discipline. There were many others, each with their own special traits. Despite their differences, all city-states shared similar religious beliefs. They honored the same group of gods, though they might favor one god more than another. These shared myths were told around campfires, in marketplaces, and during festivals. Stories about the gods and heroes were part of everyday life.

1.3 The Role of Geography in Myth Creation

The Greeks loved to explain the world around them through stories. If they saw a storm at sea, they imagined that the god of the sea, Poseidon, was stirring up the waters in anger. If they had a good harvest of grapes, they might thank Dionysus, the god of wine. Mountains, forests, and springs were believed to be homes of nymphs, spirits, or minor gods.

This strong link between geography and myth can be seen in place-names that honor gods or heroes. Certain mountains were believed to be the seat of powerful beings, while caves might be seen as gateways to hidden realms. Because of the region's many unique features—like hot springs, volcanic islands, and deep gorges—mythology naturally grew around them.

Greek religion was not just about temples and rituals. It was also about how people understood their surroundings. Farmers prayed to Demeter for healthy crops. Sailors prayed to Poseidon for safe voyages. These beliefs united communities, and they also caused fear. People worried about angering a god by doing the wrong thing or failing to offer proper thanks.

1.4 Influence of the Minoans and Mycenaeans

Before the rise of the famous city-states, there were two earlier civilizations in the area: the **Minoans** on the island of Crete and the **Mycenaeans** on the mainland of Greece. The Minoans were known for their grand palaces, such as the one at Knossos, filled with colorful wall paintings. Their art often showed people dancing, leaping over bulls, and enjoying life. We do not know all the details of their religion, but we do know they respected female figures and possibly worshipped one or more mother goddesses. They also had a script that we call **Linear A**, which we cannot fully read today.

The Mycenaeans, on the other hand, built fortress-like cities in places such as Mycenae and Tiryns. They were warriors and traders, sailing far and wide. They used a script called **Linear B**, which has been mostly decoded. It gives us some clues about their daily life, which included references to gods that resemble later Greek deities. The Mycenaeans had powerful kings and a structure that seemed to revolve around war and conquest. They might have been the people who fought in the legendary Trojan War, which is central to Greek myth.

Both the Minoans and Mycenaeans left behind stories or hints of stories that would later blend into Greek mythology. For instance, the labyrinth and the Minotaur legend may have come from the palace structures in Crete. The powerful Mycenaean kings could have inspired tales of mighty heroes who led armies against distant cities. Over time, oral traditions mixed these early myths into a larger tapestry.

1.5 Religion and Daily Life: A Close Bond

In ancient Greece, religion was part of daily life. It was not separated from politics, art, or family. People believed that gods had real power in the world, so pleasing them was important for safety and success. Temples were built to honor different gods, and festivals were held to celebrate them at certain times of the year. These festivals might include athletic contests, plays, dances, and sacrifices of animals. The meat from sacrifices was shared among people, turning the event into a community feast.

Men, women, and children each had roles in worship. Certain gods were called upon for certain needs. Women might pray to Hera for marriage or for protection of their families. Soldiers might pray to Ares for courage in battle. Farmers might pray to Demeter for fertile land. This direct connection to everyday problems made religion an active force. People would place small offerings in temples, such as fruit, wine, or small clay figures. In return, they hoped for health, good weather, or victory in conflict.

The Greeks also practiced **divination**, seeking signs of the future in natural events or the behavior of birds. Oracles, such as the famous one at Delphi, were seen as a mouthpiece of the god Apollo. Visitors traveled long distances to ask questions about their future. The oracles would give cryptic answers that often needed interpretation. This custom shows the level of trust people placed in communication with the gods.

1.6 Storytelling Traditions

Greek myths were passed down mainly through spoken word before they were written down. Poets and bards wandered from one settlement to another, performing in gatherings and public events. They played a stringed instrument called the lyre, adding musical elements to the storytelling. These performances could last hours or even days. People would sit around a fire or in an open courtyard, listening and sharing in the tales.

Because of this oral tradition, stories could change over time, and details might vary from one region to another. Yet the core elements remained: gods, heroes, monsters, and moral lessons. Myths explained why the world was as it was, and they also offered examples of how people should act. Heroes showed qualities like bravery, cleverness, and sometimes humility, though they often had flaws as well.

Homer, the poet credited with the **Iliad** and the **Odyssey**, played a huge role in fixing certain stories in the Greek mind. Though he probably drew on older tales, his epics about the Trojan War and the journey of Odysseus became a shared literary heritage. Children in many Greek city-states learned parts of Homer's poems by heart. They saw in these stories a reflection of their own hopes and fears.

1.7 Importance of Competition and Festivals

Competition was a big part of ancient Greek life. The land was divided into many city-states, and these states often competed in warfare, but they also held friendly rivalries in sports and the arts. The Olympic Games, which started in Olympia, were held in honor of Zeus. Athletes from different regions gathered to compete in running, wrestling, and other events. Victors were praised as heroes in their home city-states, and they sometimes received free meals for the rest of their lives.

Besides the Olympic Games, there were other festivals like the Pythian Games at Delphi, the Isthmian Games near Corinth, and the Nemean Games. These events tied to religious celebrations and honored different gods. It was a chance for Greek people from many cities to meet peacefully, share news, and trade. The spirit of competition also extended to drama and poetry contests during festivals like the Dionysia in Athens, dedicated to Dionysus, the god of wine and theater.

Because the gods were believed to take interest in human events, people felt that winning a contest was a sign of favor from the divine. This merged religion with athletic and artistic competitions, strengthening the sense that the gods watched over all aspects of life.

1.8 Cultural Exchange and Colonization

As Greek sailors and traders roamed the seas, they came into contact with other cultures, such as the Phoenicians and the Egyptians. They picked up ideas, goods, and new stories, weaving them into their own myths. Over time, some city-states became crowded or faced food shortages. This led to the founding of **colonies** around the Mediterranean and Black Seas. People left their home city-state under the guidance of a leader, hoping to find fertile land abroad. Once established, these colonies maintained ties with their mother city, sharing religious festivals and sometimes sending goods back and forth.

In setting up these colonies, the Greeks spread their language and culture to distant coasts. They built temples to the Greek gods and told Greek stories, but they also adapted to local customs. This mingling of ideas helped Greek mythology grow wider in scope. It also gave them new heroes and new legends, shaped by encounters with different environments.

Through colonization and trade, the power of certain city-states grew. Wealthy merchants sponsored festivals and built large homes. Craftsmen became more skilled, creating famous styles of pottery with painted scenes of myths. All of this created a backdrop for the continued telling and retelling of mythological tales.

1.9 The Seeds of Greek Philosophy

Although early Greek thinkers are often celebrated for their fresh ideas about the universe, it is important to note that these ideas emerged from a backdrop of myth. Before people asked philosophical questions like "What is the nature of reality?" or "What is the source of all things?" they had a rich tradition of myths explaining the same phenomena. Over time, some thinkers started looking for natural explanations for storms, earthquakes, and other events. They still respected the gods, but they also wondered if there might be basic elements like fire, water, air, or earth that made up the world.

These early ideas did not replace myths for most people; rather, they existed alongside them. Common folk still believed in the direct influence of gods on daily life, while certain philosophers proposed that knowledge could come from careful observation or logical reasoning. This shows how layered ancient Greek culture was: an ordinary farmer might pray to Zeus for rain one day, while a traveling teacher might discuss the principles of the cosmos the next. Both ways of thinking contributed to the larger tapestry of Greek civilization.

1.10 Lasting Impact on the Mythic Imagination

The daily life and landscape of ancient Greece shaped its myths in a big way. The closeness to the sea, the jagged mountains, the limited farmland, and the constant interactions among city-states helped form a worldview where gods were powerful yet near. Heroes emerged to explain acts of bravery or the founding of certain cities. Monsters might represent fears of the unknown, from the deep ocean to dark caves in the mountains.

Because the Greeks faced real challenges—like scarce farmland, rival city-states, and sudden storms at sea—the myths often present gods who can be both generous and cruel. One day they might bless a harvest or guide a hero to victory; the next day they might punish prideful leaders or unleash monsters to teach humility.

Stories about creation, war, and love all reflect the hopes and fears of these early city-states. As you continue reading, you will see these connections grow clearer. Different city-states contributed their own local legends, turning Greek mythology into a wide-ranging collection of tales. Each story teaches something about human nature, life's hardships, and the longing for guidance from powers beyond ourselves.

CHAPTER 2

The Birth of the Gods

2.1 Introduction to Greek Creation Myths

The ancient Greeks tried to explain the origin of the world and the gods through a set of stories that start with Chaos. In Greek, **Chaos** meant a vast emptiness or void—like a dark, yawning space where nothing yet existed. There was no earth, sky, or sea. Over time, from this emptiness, certain powerful beings came into being. Their arrival brought shape and definition to the universe.

These earliest beings are different from the later gods like Zeus or Hera. They are more like elemental forces or primal deities. They do not always have clear personalities, but they set the groundwork for all other myths. By telling stories of how the universe began, the Greeks tried to make sense of things like why the sun rises or why life ends in death.

2.2 Chaos and the First Beings

Out of Chaos emerged **Gaia** (Earth), **Tartarus** (the deep region beneath the earth), and **Eros** (the force of love or attraction). Different Greek sources mention other beings too, like **Erebus** (darkness) and **Nyx** (night). But the key figure here is **Gaia**, the Earth, because she becomes the mother of many powerful gods and monsters. Gaia represents the solid ground under everyone's feet, and in mythology, she is both an actual goddess and a symbol of the planet itself.

Tartarus is often described as a deep pit or the darkest part of the world. Later myths say that the wicked are punished there, and that it is even lower than Hades, the usual realm of the dead. Eros, on the other hand, symbolizes the attraction that draws beings together to create new life. This sets the stage for the births of gods, Titans, and other creatures. Love or attraction is essential for growth and for forming connections among deities.

In these myths, creation was not made by one all-powerful figure. Instead, it unfolded naturally through relationships. The Greeks did not have a single creation event by a supreme being. They believed that each divine force appeared and then interacted to produce the next generation. This idea of generations—where each new group of gods is born from an older group—runs through all Greek mythology.

2.3 Gaia and Uranus

Gaia, the Earth, brought forth **Uranus**, the sky. Sometimes Uranus is said to be born by Gaia alone; other times it is said that Uranus also came from Chaos. Either way, Gaia and Uranus became partners, embracing to form a union of earth and sky. Their bond was fruitful, leading to many children. These included the **Titans**, the **Cyclopes**, and the **Hecatoncheires** (also called the Hundred-Handed Giants).

The Titans are often described as strong and majestic. Some of their names are **Oceanus**, **Coeus**, **Crius**, **Hyperion**, **Iapetus**, **Theia**, **Rhea**, **Themis**, **Mnemosyne**, **Phoebe**, **Tethys**, and the youngest, **Cronus**. The Cyclopes were huge, one-eyed beings who would later help shape the thunderbolts for Zeus. The Hecatoncheires were gigantic beings with a hundred hands and fifty heads, symbolizing great natural forces.

Though these children were mighty, Uranus feared them. He saw them as threats to his own place as ruler of the skies. Some myths say he disliked their monstrous forms. Others say he was simply afraid of their potential. Whichever reason, Uranus decided to trap them, forcing them to stay within Gaia's body or in hidden places. Gaia grew angry at Uranus for imprisoning their children, and she began to plot against him.

2.4 Cronus and the Plot Against Uranus

Gaia, eager to free her children, created a special sickle made of the hardest stone. She called on each child to help her stand against Uranus. All were frightened, but **Cronus**, the youngest Titan, stepped forward. With Gaia's guidance, Cronus set a trap. When Uranus approached Gaia in the night, Cronus used the sickle to strike and wound his father, weakening him. This act forced Uranus to retreat, opening space for the Titans to emerge more freely into the world.

The story of Cronus's revolt shows an important theme in Greek mythology: the cycle of offspring challenging and overthrowing their parents. It is not a gentle passing of power but often a violent or dramatic event. This sets the pattern for what will happen with Cronus and his own children later.

After the confrontation, bits of Uranus's essence fell onto the earth or into the sea. Myths say that from these drops came new beings, such as the **Erinyes** (the Furies) who punished those who broke certain moral laws, and **Aphrodite**, the goddess of love, who rose from the sea foam. This birth story of Aphrodite is told in more than one version, but in many texts, she comes from the foam created by Uranus's fall. This moment is a reminder that even violent acts can lead to the creation of new life and new deities in Greek myths.

2.5 The Age of the Titans Under Cronus

With Uranus no longer ruling, Cronus and his siblings became the dominant forces in the world. Cronus took charge, becoming the leader of the Titans. He married his sister **Rhea**, and they ruled over a golden age—an era that people later remembered as one of prosperity. During this golden age, the earth supposedly produced plenty of food without human labor, and there was no war or strife.

But Cronus carried the same fear that plagued Uranus: the fear of being overthrown by his own offspring. He had heard a prophecy that one of his children would rise against him. To prevent this, Cronus decided to swallow each child as soon as they were born. One after another, he swallowed **Hestia**, **Demeter**, **Hera**, **Hades**, and **Poseidon**, keeping them locked inside him so they could not grow strong and challenge his rule.

Rhea was horrified by this. When she was pregnant with her next child, **Zeus**, she sought Gaia's help. Gaia advised her to give Cronus a swaddled stone instead of the baby. Cronus, thinking it was his newborn, swallowed the stone. Meanwhile, the real Zeus was hidden away and cared for in a secret place, often said to be a cave on the island of Crete. There, Zeus grew up, nourished by the milk of a divine goat named **Amalthea**.

This deception set the stage for Cronus's eventual downfall. Zeus, once grown, would return to free his siblings and wage war against the Titans. The pattern of father against son repeated itself. The prophecy that Cronus tried so hard to avoid in the end came true, just as Uranus's fears had come true. This theme of fate is central in Greek myths: no matter how hard someone tries to escape a destiny revealed by prophecy, they often end up causing that fate themselves.

2.6 Zeus's Return and the Potion of Metis

When Zeus reached adulthood, he began his plan to defeat Cronus. In some stories, the goddess **Metis**, known for her wisdom, helped Zeus. She gave Cronus a potion that forced him to vomit up the children he had swallowed. The siblings emerged, fully grown and ready to follow Zeus in battle. The stone Cronus swallowed instead of Zeus was also spat out and eventually became a famous object of worship at the oracle of Delphi, referred to as the **Omphalos Stone** (meaning "navel" of the earth).

Freed and furious, Zeus's siblings joined him against Cronus and the other Titans who supported Cronus's rule. This conflict was known as the **Titanomachy**, the war between Titans and the younger gods who came to be called the **Olympians**. It was a long, fierce battle. The earth shook, the sky roared with thunder, and seas churned. Some myths say that the Cyclopes and the Hundred-Handed Giants also joined Zeus's side because Cronus had imprisoned them. Grateful for their release, the Cyclopes forged thunderbolts for Zeus, which became his signature weapon.

2.7 The Titanomachy: War in Heaven and Earth

The Titanomachy was said to last for ten years. Zeus led his siblings—Poseidon, Hades, Hera, Demeter, and Hestia—along with allies like the Cyclopes and the Hundred-Handed Giants. The Titans were led by Cronus and included some of his brothers. Some Titans, like **Oceanus**, tried to remain neutral, but most sided with Cronus out of loyalty or fear.

The battles took place across land, sea, and sky. Flames and lightning filled the heavens. Earthquakes split the ground. The Hundred-Handed Giants hurled huge boulders that crashed down onto Titan ranks. In the end, Zeus and his allies overpowered Cronus and the rebellious Titans. As punishment, Zeus locked most of the Titans away in Tartarus. A few Titans were spared, like **Atlas**, who was forced to hold up the sky, and others who did not actively oppose Zeus. The new gods, the Olympians, claimed Mount Olympus as their seat of power.

This war showed that the old order was fading and a new era was dawning. It also set the stage for how the universe would be divided among the Olympian gods: Zeus took the sky, Poseidon took the sea, and Hades took the Underworld. The earth was left shared among them all, with Demeter looking after crops and harvest, and Hestia tending to the hearth and home.

2.8 The Gigantomachy and the Threat of the Giants

After the Titanomachy, there was another major conflict called the **Gigantomachy**, involving giants born from Gaia. Some say Gaia, angry at the harsh punishment of the Titans, created the Giants to challenge the Olympians. These giants were enormous beings, sometimes depicted with snake-like legs and great strength. They tried to storm Mount Olympus by stacking mountains on top of each other.

Zeus and the other Olympians fought back, but a prophecy said that the gods could not defeat the Giants alone. A mortal hero was needed, so **Heracles** (also called Hercules) joined the battle. With his help and the combined might of the Olympians, the Giants were finally beaten. This second great war reaffirmed the Olympians as the dominant power in the cosmos and illustrated again how important prophecy and fate were in Greek myth.

2.9 The Reign of the Olympians

Once the wars were over, Zeus and his siblings established a new order. From their palaces on Mount Olympus, they governed different parts of the world. Though Zeus was the king of the gods, his rule was not always calm. The Olympians had their rivalries and quarrels. The stories of their arguments, marriages, love affairs, and punishments of mortals fill many of the myths still told today. But in terms of cosmic power, no group challenged them again as fiercely as the Titans or the Giants had.

Zeus fathered many children, both with goddesses and with mortal women. Some of these children became notable gods or heroes, such as Athena (born from Zeus's head, fully grown) and Apollo and Artemis (born from the Titaness Leto). Poseidon watched over all seas, causing earthquakes when angry. Hades ruled the Underworld, rarely leaving his gloomy domain. Hera, Zeus's sister and wife, became the queen of the gods, known for her jealousy and her role as the guardian of marriage. Demeter looked after agriculture, ensuring crops grew for humans. Hestia tended the sacred flame, which symbolized the warmth of family and community.

2.10 Themes of Fate and Generational Conflict

A major theme in these creation stories is the struggle between generations. Uranus feared his children, Cronus feared his children, and each time, the prophecy of a child rising up came true. This reflects an old Greek belief that power is never guaranteed and that trying to avoid fate often leads to fulfilling it. Another theme is the idea that creation is not a single event but a process of many births, battles, and alliances.

These myths show that even gods have weaknesses, fears, and flaws. They can be tricked, they can feel jealousy, and they can be overthrown. This made the Greek gods different from the idea of a perfect, all-knowing creator. Instead, the Olympians are powerful yet human-like in their emotions. Their stories were meant to explain the forces of nature, the cycles of life, and the moral lessons about arrogance and humility.

2.11 The Influence of Hesiod

Much of our knowledge of these early stories comes from the poet **Hesiod**, who wrote **Theogony**. This work describes the genealogy of the gods and recounts the tale from Chaos to the reign of Zeus. Hesiod was trying to put into a single poem the many myths that existed in different parts of Greece. While he did not create these stories, he shaped them in a way that many later Greeks accepted as the official version.

But even in Hesiod's time, variations of these myths existed. Some regions had their own ways of telling how certain gods were born. The details might differ. One region might say Aphrodite rose from sea foam; another might link her to Zeus and Dione. Such variations were common because, for much of ancient Greek history, religion and myth were not governed by a single sacred text. Instead, local traditions thrived, and traveling poets kept them alive.

2.12 How Creation Myths Affected Daily Life

These stories were not just entertainment. They explained why people had to offer sacrifices or hold certain festivals. They also showed that the gods had once fought fiercely for control, so humans could believe that storms and natural disasters were echoes of that struggle. The fear of being punished by the gods if one acted wrongly was very real. At the same time, there was hope that if the gods were honored correctly, people would be rewarded with good harvests, calm seas, or healthy children.

The creation myths served as the foundation upon which all other stories rested. By knowing how Zeus defeated the Titans, people understood why Zeus was so powerful. By hearing about Cronus swallowing his children, they learned to respect the unstoppable nature of fate. When they saw thunderstorms, they might think of Zeus hurling his thunderbolts.

2.13 Moral Lessons in Creation Myths

While these stories might seem violent and strange, the Greeks took moral lessons from them. One lesson was that cruelty and injustice, like Uranus imprisoning his children or Cronus swallowing his offspring, lead to downfall. Another lesson was about the danger of hubris—excessive pride. When a deity or mortal tried to defy fate or rise above their station, they faced disaster. In these creation tales, even cosmic beings could not escape the consequences of their actions.

A third lesson is the cycle of power. Each ruler believed they could keep control forever, yet each eventually fell. This taught that no one should grow too comfortable or ignore warnings. Prophecies, often delivered by oracles or wise figures, were not to be dismissed. If they predicted a downfall, the best path might be humility or acceptance, not denial or force.

2.14 Transition to the Age of Mortals and the Olympians

After the Titanomachy and the Gigantomachy, the Olympians took charge. This sets the stage for the next wave of myths focusing on how gods interact with mortals. The lines between divine and human begin to blur. Some gods become parents to half-god, half-human children. Heroes like Hercules, Perseus, and Theseus emerge in later tales. These heroes carry out quests that often involve monsters left over from the earlier ages or tasks assigned by the gods.

Humans in these myths sometimes worship the Olympians with great devotion, hoping for protection or favor. Sometimes, they suffer when gods argue among themselves. The Greeks saw the gods as powerful but also flawed, which helped people understand the unpredictability of life. If the gods themselves argued and sometimes acted out of jealousy or anger, it explained why misfortune could strike even the faithful.

The golden age under Cronus was said to be a time when humans lived without sorrow or need, but that age was gone. With the new rule of Zeus, there came new challenges and new blessings. Work became necessary, and mortals had to strive to please the gods. The story would evolve further in the myths of Prometheus and Pandora, which explain how humans gained fire and the source of their troubles. But that is a story for another chapter.

2.15 Conclusion of Chapter 2

The birth of the gods in Greek mythology is a story about how the world took shape. It begins in emptiness and grows through acts of creation, conflict, and union. Chaos gives rise to Gaia, who produces Uranus, and from their union come the Titans, the Cyclopes, and the Hundred-Handed Giants. Cronus overthrows Uranus, but he is later challenged by his own child, Zeus. The great wars of the Titanomachy and Gigantomachy establish the reign of the Olympian gods, who will dominate the myths that follow.

These tales are essential to understanding all other parts of Greek mythology. They tell us why Zeus uses lightning bolts, why certain gods have certain domains, and why the gods can be both protective and vengeful. They also show how the Greeks perceived the universe: not as a single act of creation, but as a continuing story of births, battles, relationships, and changes in leadership.

CHAPTER 3

Cronus and the Titans

3.1 Introduction to the Titan Age

When most people hear about Greek mythology, they often think of gods like Zeus or Athena. But before Zeus and the Olympians ruled, there was an older generation of gods called the **Titans**. They were the children of Gaia (Earth) and Uranus (Sky), and they held great power over different parts of the world. The Titan Age is sometimes called the **Golden Age**, because later generations remembered it as a time when the earth provided food without hard labor and when people supposedly lived in peace. This view, however, might be an idealized memory. The Titans themselves experienced conflict, betrayal, and fear, much like the gods who followed.

The most famous Titan is **Cronus**, the youngest of his siblings. He became the leader after he overthrew his father, Uranus. Yet Cronus's rise to power did not guarantee him a peaceful reign. Like his father before him, Cronus worried about losing his throne. This anxiety pushed him to commit harsh acts that shaped the next phase of mythology. By looking more closely at Cronus and the Titans, we see that the power struggles of gods often mirror the worries and ambitions found in human societies.

In this chapter, we will explore the origins of the Titans, the personality and deeds of Cronus, the relationships among the siblings, and how the **Titan Age** set the stage for the Olympian gods. Although some details overlap with what we have learned so far, here we expand on the daily life under the Titans, the specific roles of Cronus's brothers and sisters, and the cultural lessons the ancient Greeks drew from these early myths.

3.2 The Children of Gaia and Uranus

Gaia (Earth) and Uranus (Sky) produced a remarkable family. First, they had the twelve Titans: six male (Oceanus, Coeus, Crius, Hyperion, Iapetus, and Cronus) and six female (Theia, Rhea, Themis, Mnemosyne, Phoebe, and Tethys). Alongside these Titans, they also had the **Cyclopes**—giant one-eyed smiths—and the **Hecatoncheires** or Hundred-Handed Giants. Each new generation was strong, but the Titans stood out for their more god-like appearance and broader influence.

Among all the Titans, Cronus was the youngest male. Sometimes, being the youngest can mean weaker status, but Cronus was clever and bold. When Uranus locked away some of his children deep in the earth, Cronus was the one who took action. He ambushed his father with a stone sickle given to him by Gaia and wounded Uranus, forcing him to retreat. This violent moment led to Cronus becoming the leader of the Titan generation.

Some legends say that after Uranus was overthrown, the blood that fell on Gaia gave rise to other mythical beings, including the **Erinyes** (Furies) and the **Giants**. In this sense, the brutality of that act did not just end Uranus's control; it also created new forces in the world. Cronus's actions marked the end of one era and the start of another. Yet the seeds of conflict were planted, for Cronus used violence to gain power, and such power is seldom held without a price.

3.3 Cronus's Personality and Leadership

Cronus is often depicted as a complex figure. On the one hand, he brought freedom to his siblings when he defeated Uranus, removing the father's oppressive rule. On the other hand, Cronus himself repeated a similar pattern of control and fear when he came into power. Myths describe Cronus as paranoid, always looking over his shoulder for threats—even within his own family.

Unlike Zeus, who later became known for giving roles to his siblings and establishing a certain level of cooperation, Cronus did not seem interested in sharing authority. He married his sister **Rhea**, but he did not create a stable ruling council. Instead, he focused on maintaining his own supremacy, ignoring the possibility of delegating significant tasks or trusting others.

Cronus represents the concept of **time** in some interpretations of Greek myth (he is sometimes mixed up with Chronos, a personification of time, though they are not exactly the same figure). Still, the idea of Cronus as a devouring force that destroys even what he creates fits the theme of time's unstoppable nature. He fathered several children, but because of a prophecy that one child would overthrow him, he chose to swallow them at birth, preventing them from growing to challenge him.

3.4 The Twelve Titans: A Closer Look

While Cronus was the central Titan, the others each had traits and domains worth noting. Though the details are not always as developed as those of the Olympian gods, they formed the background against which Cronus ruled:

- **Oceanus**: He was linked to the great river that was believed to surround the earth. Together with his sister Tethys, he fathered many river gods and sea nymphs known as Oceanids.
- **Tethys**: As the consort of Oceanus, she was a mother of sea creatures and freshwater springs.

- **Hyperion**: Sometimes associated with heavenly light; father of Helios (the sun), Selene (the moon), and Eos (the dawn).
- **Theia**: Partner of Hyperion; mother of the celestial bodies mentioned above.
- **Coeus** and **Phoebe**: Linked to intellect and possibly oracular power. Phoebe was sometimes tied to the moon in certain traditions, though these roles often overlapped or changed in different regions.
- **Crius**: Lesser known in the myths, but sometimes connected to constellations or the four corners of the earth.
- **Iapetus**: Father to notable figures like Prometheus and Atlas. These children would play critical roles in later tales.
- **Themis**: The Titaness of divine law and order; mother of the Horae (seasons) and the Moirai (Fates) in some versions.
- **Mnemosyne**: The personification of memory; mother of the nine Muses with Zeus in later myths.
- **Rhea**: Sister and wife of Cronus, mother of the first Olympians like Hestia, Demeter, Hera, Hades, Poseidon, and Zeus.

Each Titan was powerful, and in some stories, they held dominion over certain realms—light, water, memory, or prophecy. However, the Greeks eventually placed more importance on the Olympian gods, so we have fewer tales of the Titans interacting with mortals directly. The Titans belong to a more primeval period, when the lines between nature and deity were not as clearly drawn. They were, in a sense, living embodiments of large cosmic forces.

3.5 Daily Life in the Golden Age

During the early reign of Cronus, mortals experienced what they called the **Golden Age**. It was said that people did not have to work the fields, for the earth produced enough food on its own. There were no wars, and nobody grew old in misery. Death came gently, almost like sleep. Whether this was a literal belief or a poetic way of describing a distant past, the myth carries a message: before the complexities of later eras, life was simpler and more harmonious.

From a cultural perspective, the Golden Age might reflect the idea that ancient people lived closer to nature, with fewer conflicts or social structures. Some poets describe this time as free from worry, highlighting how humans lived in harmony with the environment. Yet, from a mythic standpoint, this age was overshadowed by Cronus's actions toward his own offspring. While humans might have enjoyed a peaceful existence, the Titan family was anything but calm.

What made this age "golden" for mortals might not have been true for the gods themselves. Cronus's fear of being overthrown meant that he did not experience the same harmony that mortals supposedly did. He devoured his children one by one—Hestia, Demeter, Hera, Hades, and Poseidon—showing that even in a so-called perfect time, there can be darkness hidden behind the scenes.

3.6 Rhea: Mother of the First Olympians

Rhea, like her mother Gaia, is a nurturing figure. She saw her children swallowed by Cronus and felt powerless to stop him. Finally, when she was pregnant with **Zeus**, Rhea devised a plan to trick her husband. She secretly gave birth to Zeus in a hidden cave, often said to be on the island of Crete. Different local myths mention nymphs or goat-like creatures (such as the goat Amalthea) who cared for the infant god.

To fool Cronus, Rhea wrapped a stone in swaddling clothes and presented it to him as the newborn child. Cronus, paranoid and quick to act, swallowed the stone without noticing the deception. In this way, Rhea saved Zeus from her husband's hunger. Her bravery and cunning set in motion the events that would topple Cronus and bring about the next generation of deities.

Rhea's actions show the strength of maternal love and the willingness to oppose cruelty, even if it meant betraying the king of the Titans. Once Zeus grew up in secret, he returned to free his siblings, fulfilling the very prophecy Cronus had worked so hard to avoid.

3.7 Cultural Lessons: Fear and Tyranny

The story of Cronus swallowing his children is one of the most striking images in Greek mythology. It is gruesome yet teaches several lessons. First, it emphasizes that excessive fear—especially fear of losing power—leads to actions that ultimately ensure one's downfall. By trying to control every possible threat, Cronus created the very situation in which he would eventually fail.

Second, it shows that injustice done to one's own family often has serious consequences. Cronus's behavior was not just harsh; it was a betrayal of natural bonds. This betrayal would not be forgotten by his children, who emerged fully grown and ready to seek justice.

Lastly, there is an underlying lesson about fate. No matter how hard Cronus tried to escape the prophecy, he ended up fulfilling it. This belief in unchangeable destiny appears again and again in Greek myths, reminding us that efforts to avoid fate often bring it about more certainly.

3.8 Hidden Acts of Defiance Among the Titans

While Cronus tried to remain in command, some of his siblings had their own thoughts and agendas. Not all Titans agreed with the way Cronus managed his rule. For instance, **Oceanus** seemed content to remain in his watery domain, not directly helping or opposing Cronus. **Themis** and **Mnemosyne** later sided with Zeus, or at least cooperated with him when the great war—known as the **Titanomachy**—began. It can be guessed that Cronus's actions caused quiet unrest among the Titans.

However, the Titans did not openly confront Cronus until Zeus matured and launched a challenge. The reasons might include fear of Cronus's power or a lack of unity among the Titans themselves. Each Titan had his or her own domain, and while they respected Cronus as the leader, they were not necessarily eager to join in a bloody conflict without a clear outcome. This division within the Titan ranks gave Zeus a possible advantage later.

Such subtle tensions paint a picture of a court held under a strict ruler: many obey out of fear, while others seek neutrality or wait for a better leader to emerge. Cronus may have seen control as the key to stability, but the seeds of rebellion were already sown, both among the Titans and in the fate of his own children.

3.9 The Role of Gaia in Cronus's Downfall

Gaia, the Earth, was the mother of the Titans and often associated with nurturing life. She first helped Cronus overthrow Uranus because she was angry about Uranus imprisoning her children. But once Cronus proved to be just as cruel in his own way, Gaia grew dissatisfied with him as well. When Rhea sought help to save Zeus, Gaia provided counsel and protection, reflecting her ongoing desire to see her descendants live free.

Gaia's shifting loyalties show that she did not blindly support any single ruler. Instead, she acted in line with her maternal instincts and sense of justice, punishing those who misused power. In some stories, Gaia's role continues beyond Cronus's defeat: she later gives birth to the **Giants** to challenge Zeus if she feels the Olympians are too harsh. This cycle of divine parenting, rebellion, and punishment repeats throughout Greek mythology, echoing the complex relationships in families and governments alike.

3.10 Growing Suspicion and the Seeds of War

From the moment Zeus was saved, Cronus had reason to worry. He may not have known exactly what Rhea had done, but Cronus was not naive. Myths do not describe him as blind to possible plots. Nevertheless, his paranoia had already led him to extreme measures. What else could he do? The prophecy warned of a son who would dethrone him, and Cronus had tried his best to stop that son from existing.

Zeus, meanwhile, was raised in secrecy, learning not just survival but also strategy. When the time was right, Zeus returned to confront Cronus, aided by Metis, the goddess of wisdom or thought in some versions. The plan was to make Cronus drink a potion that forced him to vomit up the swallowed children. Hestia, Demeter, Hera, Hades, and Poseidon emerged fully formed, furious at their father. They joined Zeus in what would become a cosmic showdown known as the **Titanomachy**.

This battle was not only about power; it was about the future shape of the cosmos. If Cronus won, the Titan rule would continue. If Zeus and his siblings succeeded, the Olympian era would begin. Many Titans supported Cronus, but some remained neutral or even helped Zeus in secret. The Cyclopes and the Hundred-Handed Giants, long ago imprisoned by Uranus and then by Cronus, sided with Zeus after he freed them. Their support turned the tide in the coming war.

3.11 Life Under Cronus's Rule: Myth vs. Reality

Ancient sources sometimes contradict each other about how peaceful life under Cronus truly was. One tradition calls it the Golden Age, a time of no war and no work, but another tradition highlights the darkness of Cronus's fear-driven tyranny. These contradictions can coexist in myth because myths were not written by a single author; they evolved over centuries with many local variations and poetic embellishments.

For ordinary Greeks hearing these stories, the Titan Age might have sounded like a fairy tale of innocence that got broken by the harsh reality of power struggles. Alternatively, it could serve as a cautionary tale that even a supposed paradise can be destroyed by the greed or paranoia of rulers. The truth is that Greek myths often carry more than one message, leaving listeners to draw their own lessons.

Some city-states, like Athens, held festivals such as the **Kronia**, honoring Cronus in a celebratory way, focusing on the memory of the Golden Age. During this festival, social roles were temporarily relaxed, and slaves and free citizens mingled more freely—mirroring that idea of an equal and easy society. Even though Cronus had a grim side in the myths, the Greeks still acknowledged his place in the cosmic family and recognized him through ritual.

3.12 The Moral Dimension: Love, Fear, and Family

Cronus's story is also a family saga. Gaia, the grandmother, helps Cronus against Uranus, and then helps Zeus against Cronus. Rhea, the mother, has to hide her children from the father who devours them. The children themselves, once rescued, form an alliance to overthrow the father. The raw emotions are universal: fear of losing power, love for offspring, resentment against cruelty, and the desperate courage to change one's fate.

In daily life, the Greeks saw family as a complex bond. Fathers held authority, mothers nurtured, and children were expected to respect their parents. Yet, if a father was too oppressive, tension and rebellion might arise. In mythic form, these conflicts appear magnified. Instead of mere family arguments, we get cosmic wars that reshape the universe. The moral lesson is that a family must balance authority and care; if either goes to an extreme, destruction follows.

3.13 Cronus in Later Traditions

Even after the Olympians took control, Cronus remained part of the mythic landscape. In some stories, after being overthrown, Cronus was sent to rule over the **Isles of the Blessed**, where certain heroic souls found reward in the afterlife. In another version, Cronus was simply imprisoned in Tartarus with other Titans. Poets and playwrights sometimes used Cronus as a symbol of a lost golden past or as a warning figure about the perils of tyranny.

Over time, Greek thinkers started blending Cronus with the concept of **Chronos** (Time), though the two were originally distinct. This merging happened partly because the words are similar and partly because Cronus devoured his children, much like time consumes all things. Philosophers also used the myth to illustrate that time eventually leads to change, no matter how strong a ruler or system seems.

3.14 Why Titans Matter to Greek Mythology

The Titans represent the bridge between the raw, elemental world of creation and the more familiar world of the Olympians. Their age is when cosmic forces first took on personalities but had not yet been refined into the more "human-like" gods. Studying the Titans helps us understand the foundations of Greek myth and how the Greeks saw the universe evolving through stages.

Cronus's narrative specifically touches on themes of overthrow, generational conflict, and the cyclical nature of power. These themes return in many heroic stories. For instance, mortal kings or strong warriors might try to defy prophecies, only to cause their own downfall. The Titan stories set the pattern: the older generation tries to hold on, the younger generation fights for a place, and destiny moves forward regardless of anyone's wishes.

3.15 The Path to the Titanomachy

Eventually, the tension between Cronus and his grown children reached a breaking point. Zeus, Poseidon, Hades, Hera, Demeter, and Hestia prepared to confront their father. Each possessed divine gifts and a sense of justice, believing that Cronus's reign of fear should end. Some Titans, such as Themis and Mnemosyne, quietly supported the new generation, recognizing that Cronus had gone too far.

Cronus was not without allies. Titans like Iapetus, Hyperion, and Coeus joined him, perhaps out of a sense of loyalty or because they worried about the unknown rule of a younger god like Zeus. The lines were drawn. A conflict that would shake the very roots of the earth was about to begin. Neither side could retreat without losing all hope of ruling the cosmos.

In the chapters ahead, we will see how this epic battle, the **Titanomachy**, unfolds. For now, it suffices to say that the outcome of this war would decide the shape of Greek religion and myths for centuries to come. Cronus would not give up easily, and Zeus had to prove himself worthy of leading a new order.

3.16 A Glimpse at Titan Worship in Ancient Greece

While the Olympian gods became more dominant over time, early Greeks did offer prayers and sacrifices to Titans, especially in local cults. Some shrines existed for Rhea, especially as a mother goddess. Kronia festivals in Athens honored Cronus with feasting and temporary role reversals. People recognized Cronus's importance, at least as a reminder of the mythic past, even if they did not see him as a personal protector in the same way they saw Zeus or Athena.

These festivals showed that Greek religion was not fixed by a single doctrine. It was flexible, often shaped by local traditions. Certain villages might have their own stories claiming descent from a Titan or might hold a special festival celebrating the Titan age's bounty. Over time, these practices either evolved or were absorbed into worship of the Olympians.

3.17 Lessons and Reflections on Cronus

The tale of Cronus warns against cruelty and the abuse of power. It also illustrates that fear can destroy families and realms from within. Had Cronus raised his children with care instead of swallowing them, he might have coexisted with them peacefully. Instead, his terror turned them into enemies. At the same time, Cronus's story underlines the Greek belief in fate. No matter how extreme his actions, he could not avoid the child who would eventually dethrone him.

The presence of strong female figures like Gaia and Rhea highlights the ongoing role of maternal power. Women in Greek mythology often act when male deities become too oppressive or arrogant. Their cunning and determination can change the course of events.

CHAPTER 4

The Rise of the Olympians

4.1 Introduction

Cronus's grip on power began to waver the moment he swallowed the stone instead of Zeus. In secret, Zeus grew strong and wise, determined to free his siblings and restore balance to the cosmos. This chapter focuses on the **Titanomachy**, the great war between the Titans led by Cronus and the younger gods who would become known as the Olympians under Zeus's leadership. It also explores how, after the conflict, the victorious gods established a new order, dividing the realms among themselves and shaping the world of myth as most people know it today.

The rise of the Olympians did not happen overnight. It required alliances, bravery, and sometimes cunning. Forces that had once been victims—like the Cyclopes and the Hundred-Handed Giants—played crucial roles in tipping the balance. In the end, this war was more than a family feud; it was a cosmic battle that determined who would govern the sky, the sea, the underworld, and beyond. Let us dive into the key events and see how Zeus and his siblings claimed their thrones on Mount Olympus.

4.2 Preparing for War

Zeus was raised far from his father's watchful eyes, often said to be in a cave on Crete or a remote mountainous region. There, he developed a sense of strategy and learned about Cronus's history of violence. Determined to rescue his siblings, he returned when he came of age. According to some stories, he first tricked Cronus into drinking a potion crafted by **Metis**, the goddess of clever thought. Cronus was forced to vomit up the children he had swallowed—Hestia, Demeter, Hera, Hades, and Poseidon.

Suddenly, Cronus faced five angry deities who had matured in his belly, along with Zeus, the child he had failed to devour. This event was a massive shift in power. No longer was Cronus the unquestioned ruler of the cosmos. Zeus, Hades, Poseidon, and the three goddesses were free, eager to bring justice to their father.

The newly freed siblings gathered allies where they could. They reached out to **Gaia**, who guided them as she had once guided Cronus. They also released the **Cyclopes** and the **Hundred-Handed Giants** from captivity, offering them freedom in exchange for their support. The Cyclopes, grateful, forged thunderbolts for Zeus, a powerful trident for Poseidon, and a helm of darkness for Hades. These divine weapons would prove decisive in the coming battles.

4.3 Lines Are Drawn: Titans vs. Olympians

Cronus, stunned but not defeated, rallied his Titan brothers and sisters. Some Titans, like **Coeus**, **Hyperion**, and **Iapetus**, stayed loyal to Cronus, believing that the older generation should remain in power. Others, like **Themis** and **Mnemosyne**, either remained neutral or quietly sided with Zeus, sensing that Cronus's reign was doomed. **Oceanus** seemed more interested in keeping peace and did not engage heavily on either side, though different versions of the myth vary on his involvement.

The war was named the **Titanomachy**, signifying a battle of titanic proportions. Skirmishes took place across the land, in the sky, and even in the seas. The Olympians set up their base on Mount Olympus, a high peak that later became known as their realm. Cronus and his Titan allies occupied Mount Othrys in some stories. The conflict raged for years, each side refusing to yield. The earth trembled, volcanoes erupted, and lightning lit the skies. It was said that the noise of battle could be heard from one end of creation to the other.

4.4 The Role of the Cyclopes and Hundred-Handed Giants

One key factor in the Olympian victory was the aid of the **Cyclopes** and the **Hecatoncheires** (Hundred-Handed Giants). Under Cronus, these powerful beings had been locked away, just as Uranus had once done. By releasing them, Zeus gained mighty allies who harbored deep resentment toward Cronus. Their strength, combined with the Olympians' cunning and new weapons, gave Zeus's side an edge.

- The **Cyclopes**, with their skill in forging, created the thunderbolt (for Zeus), the trident (for Poseidon), and the helm of darkness (for Hades). These gifts amplified the new gods' powers to a fearsome degree.
- The **Hundred-Handed Giants** hurled massive boulders and fought with incredible force, overwhelming Titan defenses. Each one had fifty heads and one hundred arms, making them near-unstoppable in physical combat.

In Greek myth, the gratitude of the Olympians was seldom forgotten. Later, Zeus allowed the Hundred-Handed Giants to stand guard over Tartarus, ensuring that the defeated Titans could not escape. This arrangement showed a certain respect: the Giants, once prisoners, became wardens, a fitting role given their unmatched strength.

4.5 Ten Years of Struggle

Some accounts say the Titanomachy lasted ten full years. For a decade, neither side could achieve a decisive advantage. The Olympians had youth, determination, and the newly forged weapons. The Titans had greater numbers, age-old experience, and the backing of Cronus, who was still powerful. The earth shook under constant earthquakes, tsunamis ravaged coastlines, and wildfires burned ancient forests as the battles raged on. The natural disasters in these myths may reflect how Greeks explained earthquakes, eruptions, or storms: as echoes of this primeval war.

During these ten years, gods and Titans tested each other's resilience. Poseidon fought bravely in the seas, causing monstrous waves to crash against the Titan forces. Hades used his helm of darkness to strike unseen from the shadows. Hera, Demeter, and Hestia took on essential roles as well, though many legends focus on Zeus and his brothers. The Titanesses, like Rhea and Themis, often stood in the background, offering advice or subtle support rather than direct combat. The war was not merely brute force; it also required planning, resource allocation, and morale. Each side needed to keep faith in eventual victory.

4.6 The Turning Point

The cycle of battles seemed endless until Zeus mastered the full power of the thunderbolt. When he hurled his lightning, the skies blazed white, and thunder shook the heavens. Coupled with the Hundred-Handed Giants pelting Titan fortresses with giant rocks, the Olympians began to break through the Titan lines. Poseidon, with his trident, caused the seas to surge onto the land, cutting off Titan supply routes. Hades used his invisibility helm to slip behind enemy lines, sowing confusion and fear.

Cronus fought back fiercely, but he lacked the combined might that Zeus and his siblings had developed. One of the major differences was unity. The Olympians functioned like a close-knit team, relying on each other's strengths. Some Titans hesitated to commit fully, uncertain whether Cronus could secure victory. This uncertainty took a toll, and once Cronus's main defenses were breached, the outcome was nearly sealed.

In a final push, Zeus faced Cronus directly, unleashing a barrage of thunderbolts. The sky roared, and the Titan king could not withstand the onslaught. Realizing defeat was inevitable, Cronus fell, and the remaining loyal Titans either surrendered or fled. Mount Othrys lay in ruins, and the Titanomachy ended with the triumph of Zeus and the Olympians.

4.7 Punishing the Defeated Titans

Following their victory, the Olympians needed to decide what to do with the conquered Titans. Zeus recognized that leaving them free might lead to another uprising. On the other hand, he also knew he should not repeat the mistake of his father and grandfather by brutally imprisoning everyone without distinction. In the end, he chose to cast most of the rebellious Titans into **Tartarus**, the deepest part of the underworld, and set the Hundred-Handed Giants as guards to keep them there.

Some Titans escaped this fate. **Rhea**, the mother of the Olympians, was never an enemy to her children. **Themis** and **Mnemosyne** had either supported or at least not opposed Zeus. **Oceanus** had remained neutral, devoting himself to the great encircling river. **Prometheus** and **Epimetheus**, sons of Iapetus, had complex roles, and Prometheus in particular would become important in the myth of mankind's creation. Meanwhile, **Atlas** was singled out for punishment, forced to hold up the sky at the edge of the world.

Zeus's decisions demonstrated a more measured approach compared to Cronus's rule. The new gods believed they had the right to enforce order, but they also recognized the need to avoid repeating the same cycle of cruelty. Nonetheless, the Titan punishment was harsh, revealing that Greek myths did not shy away from the reality of eternal sentences for enemies of the new regime.

4.8 Division of Realms Among Zeus, Poseidon, and Hades

Once the war ended, the three brothers—Zeus, Poseidon, and Hades—decided how to share the cosmos:

- **Zeus** was granted dominion over the sky and all that dwells within it. He became the king of the gods, with Mount Olympus as his seat of power.
- **Poseidon** received the sea, ruling over oceans, rivers, and waters. He became the deity sailors prayed to for calm seas and safe voyages.
- **Hades** was given the Underworld, a hidden realm for the spirits of the dead. Though powerful, Hades's domain was somber, and he rarely visited the surface.

They all shared some influence over the earth itself, but Zeus's rule was considered supreme. This division reflected a balance: sky, sea, and underworld each had a guardian, and each brother had his own area to govern. The sisters—Hera, Demeter, and Hestia—took on vital roles as well: Hera became queen of the gods, Demeter oversaw agriculture and the harvest, and Hestia kept the hearth, symbol of home and family unity.

4.9 Establishing the Olympian Court

With Cronus defeated, the Olympians set up a new order on Mount
Olympus. This divine court was made up of gods who had proven
themselves loyal and essential during the war. Over time, other gods
joined their ranks, including Aphrodite, Apollo, Artemis, Athena,
Ares, Hephaestus, and Hermes—each with unique powers and
personalities. The number **twelve** is often given for the major
Olympians, but the list can vary by source.

Life on Olympus was described as joyous but also prone to internal
quarrels, love affairs, and jealousies. The Olympians feasted on
ambrosia and drank **nectar**, magical foods that kept them immortal.
They observed events on earth and sometimes meddled in mortal
affairs. The new era was more dynamic than the Titan Age. These
gods were far from perfect but were close enough to human
emotions that mortals could relate to them. In many ways, this new
order shaped ancient Greek culture: gods who showed both virtues
and flaws, making them accessible as figures of worship and
cautionary tales alike.

4.10 Significance of the Titanomachy in Greek Thought

The epic battle that allowed the Olympians to rise served as a
central point of reference in Greek myth. It explained why certain
gods held authority and why the Titans, though older, were seldom
worshipped as the main pantheon. It also reinforced a key Greek
value: the idea that even gods must earn their place through courage
and unity. Zeus and his siblings did not inherit the world peacefully;
they fought for it and proved themselves worthy through the test of
war.

Beyond the realm of religion, the Titanomachy represented natural
upheavals. Ancient Greeks might have used it to explain volcanic

eruptions, earthquakes, and dramatic weather events. The cosmic scale of the war matched the violent phenomena they saw around them. Stories about boulders being hurled or lightning bolts scorching the sky helped them personify the forces of nature in a way that was both terrifying and awe-inspiring.

4.11 Aftermath: Peace and New Challenges

Once Zeus established his rule, there was a period of relative calm. Mortals began to acknowledge the Olympians as the true gods, offering sacrifices and building temples. Yet the defeat of Cronus was not the end of challenges. Gaia, upset at how her children the Titans were imprisoned, created another threat: the **Giants**. Their war against the Olympians would be called the **Gigantomachy**, another massive struggle that tested Zeus's regime.

Nevertheless, the victory over Cronus formed the backbone of the new cosmic order. The gods now had specific roles, and they interacted with humans in myths that range from helpful guidance to severe punishment. This structure allowed the Greeks to develop a complex pantheon that explained nearly every aspect of life, from weather patterns to moral choices.

4.12 Hera, Demeter, and Hestia

While Zeus, Poseidon, and Hades claimed the major domains, the three sisters each played a crucial part in everyday life:

- **Hera**: She became Zeus's wife and the queen of the gods. She upheld marriage and family values, though her own marriage to Zeus was far from peaceful.

- **Demeter**: She cared for the harvest and the fertility of the earth. Mortals prayed to her for bountiful crops and food security.
- **Hestia**: She kept the sacred fire of Olympus and was the goddess of the hearth. Each home had a hearth dedicated to her, signifying warmth, unity, and the continuity of family life.

Their roles helped cement the Olympian order as more than just a group of warlike deities. They also oversaw aspects of life that helped civilizations thrive—family, agriculture, and communal stability. This further distinguished the Olympians from the Titans, who were less directly involved in daily human affairs.

4.13 The Role of Prophecy and Fate

The overthrow of Cronus repeated the pattern seen with Uranus. Fear of a prophecy caused a ruler to harm his offspring, yet that very act enabled the prophecy to come true. This cycle confirmed a central Greek theme: **fate** cannot be cheated. Attempts to avoid destiny usually result in fulfilling it.

The acceptance of fate shaped Greek religion and culture. People believed that even the gods bowed to certain unchangeable outcomes, symbolized by the **Moirai** (the Fates). The Titanomachy emphasized that no one, not even Cronus, could stop a predetermined course of events. In daily life, many Greeks took caution and humility from these stories, consulting oracles and paying attention to omens in hopes of aligning themselves with the will of the gods rather than opposing it.

4.14 Celebrations and Temples

After the rise of the Olympians, temples dedicated to Zeus, Hera, Poseidon, and others sprang up across the Greek world. At **Olympia**, a grand sanctuary honored Zeus with the Olympic Games. At **Delphi**, Apollo was worshipped as the god of prophecy. The city of **Athens** chose Athena as its patron deity. These places became centers of pilgrimage, reinforcing the Olympians' status as the principal gods.

Festivals celebrated the new cosmic order. For instance, the **Olympic Games** were said to be established in honor of Zeus, symbolizing the unity and shared Greek identity that the Olympian gods represented. Unlike the lesser-known cults of the Titans, the worship of Olympians became a unifying cultural force among the various city-states. Through these festivals, people expressed gratitude, sought divine favor, and retold the stories of the gods, keeping myths alive.

4.15 The Legacy of the Titanomachy

Though the Titanomachy ended with the Titans' defeat, its echoes remained in Greek stories. Some Titans were still revered in certain locales, especially those who had not fought Zeus. Others, like Atlas, appeared in new tales, holding up the sky or interacting with heroes like Heracles. The memory of the war also served as a lesson: power won through force requires wisdom to manage. The Olympians had to avoid becoming like Cronus, or they too would face rebellion.

In a broader sense, the Titanomachy set the template for other mythic conflicts. Each generation or group with power risked being replaced by the next if it grew too tyrannical. This idea resonated with the Greek view of **hubris**—excessive pride that leads to downfall. The Titanomachy was a grand demonstration of how no ruler's position is guaranteed, even among immortals.

4.16 Reflections on Family and Power

At its core, the rise of the Olympians is about a family wrestling with authority. Cronus and Zeus mirror the relationship of Uranus and Cronus: a father tries to eliminate his children out of fear, and one child fights back. The children, once freed, form a bond strong enough to overthrow the father, ending a tyrannical rule. This pattern is central to Greek mythology and reflects the ancient Greek understanding that power is a cycle, not a permanent gift.

Zeus, despite being hailed as the most just ruler among the gods, would later face his own set of challenges. Conflicts arose within his family, and mortal heroes sometimes tested his decisions. Even so, the Olympian family remained the dominant pantheon for the rest of Greek mythic tradition. Their stories, from petty arguments to grand adventures, provided a framework for how the ancient Greeks saw the world and their place in it.

4.17 The Rise of New Deities

In the aftermath of the war, new gods and goddesses began to take shape. Some, like **Aphrodite**, had earlier origins but aligned themselves with the Olympian order once it was established. Others, like **Apollo** and **Artemis** (children of Zeus and Leto), became leading figures in their own right. Each of these deities brought fresh aspects to Greek worship: music, healing, the hunt, the moon, the sun, and more.

This expansion of divine roles showed that mythic tradition did not end with the victory over Cronus. Instead, it provided fertile ground for more stories, each explaining aspects of life and nature that early Greeks found mysterious or important. The Olympians were far from perfect rulers; they quarreled, loved, and sometimes punished humans. But their complexity made them relatable and allowed for a wide variety of tales that still fascinate people today.

4.18 Transition to the Next Myths

With the cosmic structure now set—Zeus in the sky, Poseidon in the sea, Hades in the underworld—the stage was ready for myths that focus on human interaction with these gods. Heroes like **Perseus**, **Heracles**, **Theseus**, and **Jason** would undertake quests often supported or hindered by the Olympians. Love stories, tragic fates, and moral lessons would all emerge from the personalities and rivalries of the gods.

The transition from Titan to Olympian rule is the backdrop for nearly every famous Greek myth. By understanding how Zeus claimed his throne and how Cronus fell, we can see the underpinnings of each subsequent tale. We also see how the Greeks viewed divine power: it is never safe from challenge, and it must be proven in action, not simply inherited.

4.19 Lasting Importance of the Olympian Victory

The Olympian victory still resonates through Greek art, literature, and cultural memory. In Homer's epics and Hesiod's poems, references to the Titanomachy underscore the power of Zeus and his court. Greek tragedies and comedies sometimes mention the Titans as cautionary examples of what happens to those who defy the new order.

In philosophical discussions, the defeat of Cronus could symbolize the triumph of a more reasoned, ordered system over raw force and fear. Later Greek thinkers would question the moral implications of these myths, but the overall picture remained: the Olympians brought a structured world out of the chaos of war, marking a major shift from primal existence to a more civilized cosmic governance.

CHAPTER 5

The Twelve Olympian Gods

5.1 Introduction to the Olympians

After the great victory over the Titans—explored in the previous chapters—the new generation of gods claimed Mount Olympus as their home. They came to be called the **Olympians**, and they represented various forces of nature and aspects of human life. Though different lists of Olympians appear in ancient sources, most agree on **twelve** main gods. These twelve formed the core of Greek religion and appeared often in myths, worship, and festivals.

The Twelve Olympians included **Zeus**, **Hera**, **Poseidon**, **Hades** (in some traditions—though he often rules separately in the Underworld), **Demeter**, **Hestia** (sometimes replaced by or sharing a spot with Dionysus), **Aphrodite**, **Apollo**, **Artemis**, **Ares**, **Hephaestus**, **Athena**, and **Hermes**. However, Hades spent most of his time in the Underworld, so some say he is not usually counted among the "Olympian" gods who dwell in the sky. **Dionysus**, the god of wine, is another major figure sometimes listed instead of Hestia, since Hestia is a quieter deity who rarely leaves her hearth. Because ancient myths were never fixed by a single text, the exact twelve could shift.

In this chapter, we will focus on the classic group, describing each Olympian's domain, personality, symbols, and key myths. Through these gods, the ancient Greeks explained everything from storms to love to the mysteries of the harvest. Their stories reveal a society that saw divinity reflected in all parts of life, from the highest mountains to the smallest homes.

5.2 Zeus: King of the Gods

5.2.1 Domain and Attributes

Zeus is the chief deity in Greek mythology, ruling the sky and wielding the thunderbolt as his primary weapon. After overthrowing his father, Cronus, he became the leader of the Olympian gods. People looked to him for justice and order, as he was believed to punish those who lied or broke sacred oaths. His weapon, the thunderbolt, symbolized his authority over lightning and storms. When the ancient Greeks heard thunder, many believed it was a sign of Zeus's presence.

Zeus also controlled the natural laws that governed both mortals and gods. He watched over the cosmic balance, though he was far from perfect and often showed human-like flaws. Zeus could be stern and wrathful, but he could also be merciful. Greeks prayed to him for rain, good weather, and success in wars. Temples dedicated to Zeus, such as the one at Olympia, were significant religious centers where games and festivals were held to honor him.

5.2.2 Personality and Myths

Zeus was famous—or notorious—for his many relationships. He took both goddesses and mortal women as lovers, producing numerous offspring, some of whom became important gods or heroes (like Apollo, Artemis, Hermes, and Hercules). This behavior often angered **Hera**, his wife and sister, leading to quarrels on Mount Olympus. Stories of Zeus's romantic pursuits, sometimes in disguise (for example, turning into a swan, an eagle, or a bull), fill many Greek myths.

Despite his flaws, Zeus was generally seen as a protector figure—watching over guests, punishing evildoers, and upholding the laws of hospitality. Ancient Greeks felt that if a person mistreated a visitor or beggar, they were disrespecting Zeus himself. This moral aspect of Zeus's worship tied everyday ethics to divine will, encouraging kindness and fairness in social interactions.

5.3 Hera: Queen of the Gods

5.3.1 Domain and Role

Hera is the wife of Zeus and the goddess of marriage, family, and childbirth. As the queen of the gods, she is often portrayed wearing a crown and seated on a throne next to Zeus. While Zeus reigns over the sky, Hera's influence lies in upholding the sanctity of marriage and punishing unfaithfulness. She is also associated with protecting women in childbirth and guiding them through the challenges of family life.

Ancient Greeks viewed Hera as the patron of weddings and marital unions. Many couples would offer prayers to Hera, hoping for a stable, loving marriage. Temples dedicated to Hera, like those in Argos and Samos, were places where festivals celebrated her role in ensuring fertility and familial harmony.

5.3.2 Temper and Devotion

Hera's myths frequently involve her jealousy toward Zeus's numerous affairs. She often took vengeance not only on Zeus's lovers but also on the children born from those unions. One well-known example is her treatment of **Hercules**, whom she tormented throughout his life. Despite this jealousy, Hera was also revered for her steadfast protection of marriage and her nurturing side toward those who honored their vows.

Her strong temper can be seen as an extension of her devotion to marriage. She loathed disloyalty and would go to great lengths to defend her position as Zeus's wife. While some myths paint her as vindictive, others highlight her sense of justice and her willingness to stand by Zeus in times of crisis—such as during the battles against the Titans or Giants.

5.4 Poseidon: Lord of the Sea

5.4.1 Powers and Symbols

Poseidon, brother of Zeus, presides over the seas, rivers, and waters. He is usually depicted with a trident, a three-pronged spear that can stir waves, cause storms, and even shake the earth. Ancient Greeks regarded him as the god of earthquakes (hence one of his epithets, "Earth-Shaker"). Fishermen prayed to Poseidon for a bountiful catch, and sailors offered sacrifices for safe voyages.

Because the Greeks relied heavily on the sea for trade and travel, Poseidon held a place of great importance in their worship. His temperament was believed to mirror the sea itself—calm and generous one moment, then raging and destructive the next. When storms battered ships, sailors feared it might be Poseidon's wrath.

5.4.2 Rivalries and Legends

Poseidon had rivalries with other gods over the patronage of certain cities. The most famous tale involves Athens. Both Poseidon and **Athena** wanted the honor of being the city's main deity. Poseidon struck his trident into the ground, creating a saltwater spring, while Athena planted the first olive tree. The people judged the olive tree more useful, so they chose Athena, naming the city Athens in her honor.

In many myths, Poseidon fathered sea creatures, giants, and sometimes heroes. His children often reflect the wild and unpredictable nature of the sea—think of the Cyclops Polyphemus or the half-horse, half-fish hippocamps that pulled his chariot. Though overshadowed by Zeus in terms of cosmic rule, Poseidon was feared and respected for his immense power over water and land.

5.5 Hades: Ruler of the Underworld

5.5.1 Domain of the Dead

Hades, another brother of Zeus, controls the Underworld—a shadowy realm where the dead reside. Even though he is one of the most powerful gods, Hades is often not counted among the twelve because he spends nearly all his time in his subterranean domain. He is sometimes called **Pluton** (meaning "wealth") because the earth's riches—precious metals and fertile soil—come from below ground.

The Underworld is not necessarily a place of fiery torture in Greek myth; it is more like a gloomy kingdom where souls dwell after death. Hades himself is not evil, but he is grim and aloof. Mortals often feared invoking his name, worried they might attract bad luck or an untimely end. Still, he was respected as a just ruler of the dead, ensuring each soul received its proper place.

5.5.2 Persephone and the Changing Seasons

One of the central stories involving Hades is his abduction of **Persephone**, the daughter of **Demeter**. Wanting a queen, Hades took Persephone to the Underworld, causing Demeter's grief to plunge the world into barren winter. Eventually, Zeus brokered a deal that allowed Persephone to spend part of the year with her mother on the surface (spring and summer) and part of the year with Hades (fall and winter). This myth explains the cycle of seasons and highlights Hades's role in balancing life and death.

Though he rarely leaves his realm, Hades is crucial to the cosmic order. Without him, the dead would wander aimlessly. His realm holds secrets of fate, and oracles connected to the Underworld sometimes offered cryptic glimpses of the future.

5.6 Demeter: Goddess of the Harvest

5.6.1 Nurturing the Earth

Demeter, sister of Zeus, is the goddess of agriculture, grain, and fertility. Her domains are the fields and the crops that sustain human life. Ancient Greeks depended on her favor for healthy harvests, believing that without her blessing, famine could devastate entire communities. Farmers prayed and made offerings to Demeter to ensure the soil remained fertile and the weather stayed gentle for planting and reaping.

Demeter's presence is often gentle, reflecting her motherly character. She cares for mortals by teaching them how to grow and store crops, a gift that allowed civilization to develop. Large festivals like the **Eleusinian Mysteries** celebrated her role, offering participants rituals that promised spiritual renewal and a better understanding of life and death.

5.6.2 The Grief of a Mother

Demeter's love for her daughter **Persephone** becomes central in the myth of seasonal change. When Hades abducts Persephone, Demeter wanders the earth in despair, letting plants die. This period explains winter and autumn when the land lies fallow. When Persephone returns, Demeter's joy brings spring and summer's growth.

This cycle underscores Demeter's power and the importance of her emotions in the natural world. It also serves as a reminder of the deep bond between mother and child in ancient Greek culture. Some interpret this tale as a reflection of agricultural rhythms—seed underground in winter, reborn in spring.

5.7 Hestia: Keeper of the Hearth

5.7.1 Guardian of Home and Family

Hestia is the oldest daughter of Cronus and Rhea, yet she is often overlooked due to her peaceful nature. She presides over the hearth—the central fire in each household—symbolizing warmth, security, and unity. In Greek tradition, the hearth was sacred; new colonies carried a flame from the mother city's hearth to light the new settlement's fire, indicating a continuous thread of communal life.

Though not as flashy as some Olympians, Hestia was deeply respected. Families offered her a portion of every meal, ensuring she remained part of daily life. While other gods embroiled themselves in quarrels and romances, Hestia focused on keeping the home stable. Sometimes, **Dionysus** (god of wine and revelry) is said to take her place among the Twelve on Mount Olympus, but even then, Hestia's importance to domestic life never diminished.

5.7.2 Avoiding Conflict

Hestia's myths rarely involve conflict or revenge. She is often seen as the calm center of Olympus, refusing to take sides in disputes. When **Poseidon** and **Apollo** both tried to court her, she turned them down and asked Zeus to let her remain a virgin goddess, dedicated to tending the hearth. Zeus granted her this wish, showing his respect for her role in maintaining harmony.

In a pantheon where dramatic stories of battles, jealousy, and intrigue abound, Hestia stands out as a symbol of peace and domestic devotion. She taught mortals the value of togetherness and the need to nurture the family bond above all else.

5.8 Aphrodite: Goddess of Love and Beauty

5.8.1 Origins and Symbols

Aphrodite personifies love, passion, and beauty. Some myths say she was born from the sea foam near the island of Cyprus, formed when Uranus was wounded by Cronus. Others claim she is the daughter of Zeus and the Titaness Dione. Whichever story one prefers, Aphrodite's association with the sea remains a key theme, as does her overwhelming power to stir desire in gods and mortals.

Her symbols include the dove, the sparrow, and the swan—creatures associated with grace and affection. She also carries a magical girdle that can ignite love in anyone who wears or sees it. Temples built for Aphrodite stood in coastal regions, reflecting her connection to the waters from which she arose.

5.8.2 Influence and Famous Stories

Aphrodite's beauty could cause rivalry among the gods. One famous myth is the **Judgment of Paris**, where the Trojan prince Paris had to choose the fairest goddess among Hera, Athena, and Aphrodite. Aphrodite offered Paris the love of the most beautiful mortal woman, Helen of Sparta, if he declared her the winner. Paris accepted, leading to Helen's abduction and the start of the Trojan War.

While Aphrodite often represents romance and attraction, she also has a darker side when love turns to obsession or jealousy. She was married to **Hephaestus**, but she had many affairs, notably with **Ares**, the god of war. This pairing symbolizes the sometimes tumultuous link between love and conflict. Nevertheless, worshippers prayed to Aphrodite for love, fertility, and the joys of passion.

5.9 Apollo and Artemis: Twins of Light and the Hunt

5.9.1 Apollo: God of the Sun, Music, and Prophecy

Apollo is one of Zeus's sons, born to the Titaness **Leto**. He is the god of many domains: music, poetry, archery, prophecy, healing, and the sun. Often depicted with a lyre or a bow, Apollo represents harmony and clarity. He presides over the famous **Oracle of Delphi**, where his priestess, the **Pythia**, provided cryptic prophecies. Greeks traveled long distances to consult Apollo's oracle, hoping for guidance on wars, voyages, or personal matters.

In addition to prophecy, Apollo is linked to the sun, though earlier myths gave Helios that role. Over time, Helios and Apollo's sun aspects blended, with Apollo commonly called "Phoebus" (bright or radiant). Many festivals honored him, and the arts—especially music—were seen as a gift from Apollo, who was believed to inspire poets and musicians.

5.9.2 Artemis: Goddess of the Hunt and Moon

Artemis, Apollo's twin sister, is the goddess of the hunt, wild animals, childbirth, and the moon. She carries a bow and arrows, often accompanied by a deer or hunting dogs. Artemis chose to remain a maiden, dedicating herself to the wilderness and protecting young girls. She is a guardian of nature's purity, punishing those who harm it without need.

Ancient Greeks viewed Artemis as a protector of the young, ensuring safe childbirth. Yet, she could be merciless toward those who offended her or threatened the balance of nature. For instance, the hunter Actaeon accidentally saw Artemis bathing, and she transformed him into a stag that was torn apart by his own hounds. This tale highlights Artemis's strict boundaries and her role as a fierce guardian of innocence.

5.10 Ares: God of War

5.10.1 The Embodiment of Conflict

Ares, son of Zeus and Hera, represents the raw fury of war. Unlike Athena, who governs the strategic side of battle, Ares symbolizes its bloodshed, chaos, and rage. He is often shown with a spear, helmet, and shield, accompanied by personifications of Fear and Terror. Ancient Greeks had mixed feelings about Ares; while war was part of life, his impulsive, violent nature was not always admired.

Ares's worship was less widespread than that of other Olympians, possibly because the Greeks valued cunning and skill in warfare more than brute force. Nonetheless, he had temples in certain regions, like Sparta, which placed high value on martial strength. Ares's presence in myths often serves as a reminder of the darker side of conflict, contrasting with Athena's more reasoned approach.

5.10.2 Relationship with Aphrodite

One of the most famous stories about Ares is his affair with **Aphrodite**, who was married to **Hephaestus**. Hephaestus crafted a golden net to catch the pair in the act, then called the other gods to witness their shame. While some laughed, others criticized

Hephaestus for exposing the matter so openly. This story shows that not even gods of war or love could escape embarrassment and the consequences of their actions.

For mortals, Ares's presence could stir up battle frenzy, leading armies into bloody confrontations. At times, he clashed with heroes who stood for justice or cunning. The conflict between Ares and the mortal hero Diomedes during the Trojan War, for instance, showed that with divine favor and strategy, even a mortal could wound the god of war in battle.

5.11 Athena: Goddess of Wisdom and Warfare

5.11.1 Birth and Symbols

Athena is a daughter of Zeus, famously born fully grown and armored from her father's forehead after he swallowed her pregnant mother, Metis. She is the goddess of wisdom, strategy, crafts, and civilization. Unlike Ares's brute force, Athena represents disciplined, intelligent warfare. Ancient Greeks also saw her as a patron of weaving, pottery, and other crafts that advanced society.

Her symbols include the owl (representing wisdom) and the olive tree (representing peace and prosperity). The city of Athens is named for her, honoring her gift of the olive tree over Poseidon's saltwater spring. She is often shown wearing a helmet and carrying a spear and a shield decorated with the head of Medusa. This shield, called the **Aegis**, radiates fear in enemies.

5.11.2 Patron of Heroes

Heroes in Greek myths often benefit from Athena's guidance. For example, she helps **Odysseus** in his journey home after the Trojan

War, offering clever strategies to overcome obstacles. She aids **Perseus** in defeating Medusa by giving him a polished shield to safely view the Gorgon's reflection. Athena values wit, courage, and moral fortitude, rewarding those who use their intellect rather than relying on brute strength alone.

In many myths, Athena acts as a mediator, stepping in to prevent the other gods from acting rashly. Though she can be stern, she prefers negotiation and planning over thoughtless violence. Worshippers of Athena prayed for victory in battles but also for wisdom in governance, making her patron goddess of many city-states seeking both power and prosperity.

5.12 Hephaestus: God of Fire and Forge

5.12.1 The Divine Blacksmith

Hephaestus is the son of Hera (and sometimes of Zeus and Hera together). He stands out among the Olympians for his physical imperfections and skill in craftsmanship. Unlike the eternally youthful gods, Hephaestus is often depicted as lame or with a deformity in his legs. Different myths explain this: in some, Hera throws him off Mount Olympus at birth because she is ashamed of his appearance; in others, Zeus hurls him down during a quarrel.

Despite this harsh treatment, Hephaestus becomes the finest craftsman in the cosmos. He builds splendid palaces for the gods, creates Zeus's thunderbolts (with the help of the Cyclopes), and fashions magical armor. He also forges Achilles's legendary shield in the Trojan War myths. His workshop, filled with fire and metal, symbolizes the power of creation through skill and hard labor.

5.12.2 Marriage to Aphrodite and Temper

Hephaestus is married to **Aphrodite**—a union sometimes arranged by Zeus to prevent conflict among the gods who admired her. This marriage, however, is fraught with tension due to Aphrodite's extramarital affairs, especially with Ares. Hephaestus's net trap that caught them in the act is one of the best-known stories of marital strife on Olympus.

At times, Hephaestus is shown as calm and patient, but he can also display anger, especially when he feels betrayed or disrespected. His physical disability and experiences of rejection by his parents may have shaped his personality. Even so, mortals and gods alike rely on his craftsmanship, recognizing that Hephaestus's skill brings order and beauty to the world.

5.13 Hermes: Messenger and Trickster

5.13.1 Patron of Boundaries and Travel

Hermes, another son of Zeus, is the messenger of the gods, the patron of travelers, merchants, shepherds, and even thieves. He wears winged sandals (talaria) and a winged cap (petasus), allowing him to move swiftly between worlds—Olympus, Earth, and the Underworld. He carries a **caduceus**, a staff entwined with snakes, symbolizing trade, negotiation, and sometimes healing.

Hermes's role is to guide souls to the Underworld, deliver messages from the gods, and protect travelers from danger. Because he crosses boundaries, Hermes also became a symbol of transitions and change. He was worshipped at roadsides in the form of **herms**—stone pillars with a head and sometimes symbols of fertility—to mark property lines and crossroads.

5.13.2 Clever and Playful Myths

Hermes is famously clever from birth. One myth says that as an infant, he stole Apollo's cattle, then invented the lyre from a tortoise shell and offered it to Apollo as compensation. Apollo, impressed by Hermes's cunning and musical gift, forgave him. This story shows Hermes's dual nature: sly and mischievous, yet helpful and inventive.

Though he can be a trickster, Hermes also assists heroes. For example, he lends Odysseus the herb **moly** to resist the enchantress Circe, and he helps Perseus gather the items needed to defeat Medusa. Hermes's wit and mobility make him a favorite among storytellers—he is rarely still, always on the move, weaving through myths with a grin.

5.14 Dionysus: God of Wine and Ecstasy

5.14.1 Joy and Madness

Dionysus, son of Zeus and the mortal Semele, is the god of wine, revelry, and theater. He introduces wine to mortals, bringing both pleasure and chaos. Under his influence, people can feel joy, creativity, and liberation, but also lose themselves in drunken frenzy. Ancient festivals in his honor often involved processions, dances, and plays, leading to the birth of Greek theater.

Sometimes Dionysus takes Hestia's place among the twelve Olympians because his cult became incredibly popular. He represents nature's wild vitality, challenging the usual order and boundaries. His followers, known as **Maenads** or **Bacchants**, roamed forests, engaging in ecstatic rites.

5.14.2 Transformation and Redemption

Dionysus's myths focus on transformation: he can appear as a young man, a lion, or even a fierce bull. In one story, pirates who mock him find their ship filled with vines and wild animals, forcing them to jump overboard, where they become dolphins. Another story shows how Dionysus rescued his mother from the Underworld, demonstrating his power over life and death.

He also symbolizes redemption—both spiritually and socially. In certain rituals, participants sought relief from daily struggles and felt renewed. By surrendering to Dionysus's influence, they experienced freedom from worries, if only briefly. This dual nature—joy and destruction—makes Dionysus a reminder that excess can be both pleasurable and dangerous.

5.15 How the Twelve Olympians Interact

The Twelve Olympians, taken as a whole, present a family dynamic full of alliances, rivalries, and shared responsibilities. They gather on Mount Olympus to feast on ambrosia and nectar, discuss the fate of mortals, and settle disputes among themselves. Zeus usually maintains final authority, but conflicts still arise. Myths are replete with tales of disputes over mortal heroes, competition between gods for patronage of a city, or jealous rage stemming from love affairs.

This lively interplay among the gods reflects the ancient Greek view of the world: a place where many forces operate, sometimes working together in harmony and other times clashing in dramatic ways. Storms, earthquakes, love, war, harvests, and inventions are all manifestations of divine personalities, each with its own will and agenda.

5.16 Worship and Festivals

Ancient Greeks built temples, made sacrifices, and held festivals to honor each god. For instance:

- **Zeus**: Worshipped at Olympia with the Olympic Games.
- **Hera**: Celebrated in major sanctuaries like Argos and Samos.
- **Poseidon**: Prayed to by sailors before voyages, especially in coastal cities like Corinth.
- **Apollo**: Venerated at Delphi, the site of the famed oracle.
- **Artemis**: Honored in places like Ephesus, known for a large temple dedicated to her.
- **Athena**: Celebrated during the Panathenaic Festival in Athens.
- **Demeter**: Focus of the Eleusinian Mysteries near Athens.
- **Dionysus**: Central to festivals that gave rise to Greek theater.

Through these customs, each city-state formed a bond with the gods, hoping for protection and prosperity. Temples were not only places of prayer but also cultural centers, where art, poetry, and communal identity flourished. Greek religion was woven into public life, and the gods were seen as partners in every civic activity.

5.17 Lessons from the Twelve

Each Olympian teaches different lessons:

- **Zeus**: The importance of justice and the ultimate power of fate.
- **Hera**: The seriousness of marriage and loyalty, but also the harm of jealousy.
- **Poseidon**: Respect for the sea and recognition of nature's unpredictability.
- **Hades**: Acceptance of death's inevitability and the value of moral living.
- **Demeter**: Love for family, the cycles of growth and decay, and gratitude for food.
- **Hestia**: The sanctity of home and the need for inner peace.
- **Aphrodite**: The joys and perils of desire, showing how love can unite or destroy.
- **Apollo**: The pursuit of reason, art, and clarity in life.
- **Artemis**: Protection of the vulnerable and respect for nature.
- **Ares**: The reality of war's chaos, cautioning against reckless violence.
- **Athena**: Wisdom in battle and daily life, stressing intelligence over force.
- **Hephaestus**: The dignity of hard work and creativity, even under adversity.
- **Hermes**: The value of cleverness, communication, and safe journeys.
- **Dionysus** (if included): The necessity of release, passion, and renewal amid order.

These gods, with all their flaws and virtues, formed a mirror for human society. People could see aspects of themselves in the Olympians—love, anger, jealousy, generosity, and curiosity. By learning these stories, the ancient Greeks explored moral, social, and natural questions, finding in myths a reflection of their own lives.

5.18 Shifts and Variations in Ancient Times

The composition of the Twelve Olympians was not fixed. City-states or periods of history sometimes replaced one deity with another based on local preferences. For example, Hestia might step aside for Dionysus, or Hades might sometimes be included, especially if the local population emphasized the afterlife. Over centuries, Greek culture spread across the Mediterranean, merging with local gods and practices in a process known as syncretism.

Yet the central idea remained: a family of gods ruling from Olympus, each symbolizing a vital aspect of existence. This concept influenced Roman religion—where Zeus became Jupiter, Hera became Juno, and so on—spreading the worship of these gods far beyond the borders of mainland Greece.

CHAPTER 6

Mortals and the Gods

6.1 Introduction: The Delicate Relationship

In ancient Greece, humans lived in a world where the gods were constantly present—observing, influencing, and sometimes directly intervening. For the Greeks, **mortals** were not simply passive subjects of divine will. They could shape events through bravery, intelligence, and even trickery. At the same time, mortals had to respect the gods or face severe punishments for their hubris (excessive pride). This chapter explores the dynamic interplay between humans and deities in Greek mythology, showing how everyday life, epic stories, and moral lessons were all guided by the presence of the gods.

Mortals in these tales often found themselves at a crossroads. On one side was **piety**—the devotion and proper worship of the gods. On the other side was **ambition**—the desire to excel, gain glory, or challenge fate. Ancient stories warned of the dangers of ignoring divine boundaries. Yet, they also celebrated human courage and cleverness, often tested by the gods themselves.

We will look at how mortals communicated with gods, how they asked for help in personal or communal struggles, and what happened when they failed to show respect. At the same time, we will examine how some mortals rose to such fame that they became heroes, beloved—or feared—by the gods. This interplay gave Greek mythology its rich depth, where gods and men impacted each other's destinies.

6.2 Worship, Sacrifices, and Daily Devotion

6.2.1 Why Worship Mattered

In ancient Greece, religion was not a private affair—it was woven into the fabric of public life. Festivals, sacrifices, and rituals connected the community to the gods. People believed that by **honoring** the gods, they could secure blessings: good harvests from Demeter, calm seas from Poseidon, victory in battle from Ares or Athena, and so forth. If a mortal or a city neglected the gods, natural disasters or military defeats might follow. Thus, devotion was both a personal and civic duty.

Farmers might pour out libations (liquid offerings of wine or olive oil) to Demeter before planting and harvesting. Warriors sacrificed to Ares or Athena before going to war. Newlyweds invoked Hera for a stable marriage. Each god had specific preferences—Zeus might receive a white bull, Poseidon a horse or bull (due to his connection with both horses and the sea), and Artemis a deer or smaller game. These rituals were often accompanied by prayers, hymns, and sometimes feasts where the community shared roasted meat, believing the gods received their portion through the rising smoke.

6.2.2 Types of Offerings

Offerings ranged from simple tokens, like flowers and fruits, to more elaborate animal sacrifices. Wealthy individuals or city-states might dedicate statues made of precious metals, or build entire temples. At times, the grandeur of an offering reflected the seriousness of a prayer. For example, if a city was under threat from an invading army, they might slaughter many animals in a grand ceremony, hoping to appease the gods and gain their protection.

For everyday Greeks, smaller votive offerings, such as clay figurines, could be left at shrines to ask for help or show gratitude. This tradition shaped a vibrant culture of local sanctuaries and shrines spread across hillsides, crossroads, and near springs. Each location might be tied to a specific deity or local spirit, reinforcing the belief that divine power was present in every aspect of the natural world.

6.3 Communications with the Divine: Oracles and Omens

6.3.1 The Oracle of Delphi

One of the most famous ways mortals communicated with the gods was through **oracles**—individuals or sanctuaries believed to provide direct messages from deities. The **Oracle of Delphi**, dedicated to Apollo, was the most respected in the Greek world. People traveled there from far and wide to ask questions about politics, war, family matters, and more. The priestess, called the **Pythia**, would enter a trance-like state, supposedly inspired by Apollo, and speak cryptic answers.

Kings and generals often consulted Delphi before launching military campaigns. They believed the god's words could guide them to victory or warn them of defeat. However, the oracles were notoriously vague or symbolic, leaving people to interpret the divine messages in ways that sometimes led to misunderstandings.

6.3.2 Signs, Dreams, and Bird Flight

Beyond official oracles, Greeks looked for signs in everyday life—bird flight patterns, lightning strikes, or sudden gusts of wind. Such **omens** were believed to reveal a god's favor or displeasure. Dreams were another medium, as certain gods, like Hermes, could send messages while a person slept.

Diviners, known as **augurs** or **seers**, specialized in interpreting these signs. They examined the entrails of sacrificed animals or watched the sky for unusual phenomena. Although we might see these practices as superstitions, they played a central role in Greek society, influencing decisions in warfare, city planning, and even personal relationships.

6.4 The Concept of Hubris

6.4.1 Arrogance before the Gods

Hubris is a critical concept in Greek myth. It refers to excessive pride or self-confidence, especially when mortals think they are equal or superior to the gods. Such arrogance typically leads to **nemesis**—divine punishment. The Greeks believed that the gods could not tolerate mortals overstepping natural boundaries.

A famous example is the story of **Niobe**, who boasted about her fourteen children being more numerous and superior to **Leto**'s two (Apollo and Artemis). Offended, Apollo and Artemis killed Niobe's children, leaving her in such profound grief that she turned to stone. This tragic end illustrated that comparing oneself to a god—or a god's family—was the ultimate folly.

6.4.2 Punishments for Hubris

Punishments for hubris vary widely, but they typically involve losing what the mortal prized most—status, family, or freedom. The story of **Arachne** is another clear illustration. A talented weaver, Arachne boasted she could out-weave Athena. Offended by such pride, Athena challenged Arachne to a weaving contest. Though Arachne created a flawless tapestry, it depicted the gods' failings, further enraging Athena. In some versions, Athena tore Arachne's tapestry and turned her into a spider, doomed to weave forever.

These myths taught the Greeks an important lesson: know your limits, show respect to the gods, and avoid bragging about surpassing them. Even if a mortal was highly skilled, gratitude and humility were better paths than arrogance that risked divine wrath.

6.5 Gifts and Curses from the Gods

6.5.1 Boons to the Worthy

Not all interactions with the gods ended in punishment. Many mortals gained **divine gifts** or assistance for their piety and courage. For example, **Odysseus** received help from Athena because he honored the gods and demonstrated wisdom. **Perseus** got items like a reflective shield from Athena, winged sandals from Hermes, and a magic pouch to defeat Medusa.

In some cases, entire communities benefited. When the people of **Delphi** built a grand temple for Apollo, the god blessed the region, making Delphi a prosperous religious center. Gods might also appear in dreams to instruct a worthy worshipper on how to heal an illness or avoid a coming disaster, reinforcing the belief that devotion could earn tangible rewards.

6.5.2 Curses and Tragedies

On the flip side, a god offended could unleash curses that lasted generations. The House of **Atreus** exemplifies this. The family line was stained by betrayal and murder, beginning when Atreus offended the gods with gruesome actions. His sons, **Agamemnon** and **Menelaus**, faced continuous misfortune, including events leading to the Trojan War. Even after the war, curses persisted, influencing the tragedies of Orestes and Electra.

These generational curses taught that sin against the gods or heinous acts carried lasting consequences. Only profound acts of atonement or intervention by a sympathetic deity could break the cycle. This sense of inherited guilt was a powerful theme in Greek drama, reminding citizens that justice under the gods was strict and far-reaching.

6.6 Mortal Deeds That Changed the World

6.6.1 Prometheus and the Gift of Fire

One of the most famous sagas involving a mortal-like figure (technically a Titan) aiding humanity is **Prometheus**, who stole fire from the gods to give to humans. Fire symbolized knowledge, technology, and survival. By granting it to mortals, Prometheus defied Zeus's will. As punishment, Zeus chained him to a rock where an eagle devoured his liver daily, only for it to grow back overnight. This torment continued until the hero **Heracles** freed Prometheus.

Prometheus's act demonstrated compassion for humanity but also the risk of defying Olympus. The myth implies that progress often requires bold actions, and those who challenge the status quo might suffer greatly. It also sets the stage for other stories where mortals receive or steal divine knowledge, sometimes bringing them closer to the gods but also risking severe punishment.

6.6.2 Pandora's Box: The Release of Evils

In another myth tied to Prometheus's tale, **Zeus** created **Pandora**, the first mortal woman, as a form of retribution. She arrived with a sealed jar (often mistranslated as a "box") containing all evils—disease, sorrow, conflict—and one positive quality: **hope**.

When Pandora's curiosity led her to open the jar, the evils flew out into the world, afflicting mortals ever after. Only hope remained, giving humanity a reason not to surrender to despair.

This story explains why life is full of suffering but also insists that hope endures. It warns mortals about unchecked curiosity and the danger of ignoring divine warnings. Yet it also suggests that even in a world of hardship, hope is the saving grace that allows people to keep striving.

6.7 Trials of Mortals in Myths

6.7.1 The Price of Favor

Mortals who attracted a god's favor often had to prove themselves worthy. A classic example is the story of **Bellerophon**, who gained the patronage of Athena, receiving a golden bridle to tame the winged horse **Pegasus**. While this gift allowed him to perform heroic deeds like defeating the Chimera, it also fueled his ambition. Bellerophon tried to fly to Mount Olympus on Pegasus, aiming for immortality among the gods. Offended, Zeus sent a gadfly to sting Pegasus, causing Bellerophon to fall back to Earth and wander blind and crippled for the rest of his days—again, a reminder of the perils of hubris.

6.7.2 Impossible Quests

Gods sometimes set mortals on **impossible quests** to test or punish them. **King Eurystheus** forced **Heracles** to complete the Twelve Labors, many of which involved capturing or slaying deadly beasts favored by the gods. Similarly, **Jason** had to retrieve the **Golden Fleece**, navigating treacherous waters and clashing rocks with the help of gods like Hera and Athena. These trials showed mortals' reliance on divine aid and their own valor. The success or failure of these quests often revealed a mortal's character—whether they were humble or proud, persistent or easily discouraged.

6.8 Mortal Heroes and Demigods

6.8.1 Children of Gods and Mortals

Some mortals in Greek mythology are **demigods**—offspring of a god and a human. Famous examples include **Heracles** (son of Zeus and a mortal woman, Alcmene) and **Perseus** (son of Zeus and Danaë). Demigods possessed extraordinary strength or abilities, setting them apart from ordinary humans. They often performed heroic feats, sometimes assisted by their divine parent, but also faced divine enemies or challenges due to rivalries among gods.

These demigods illustrate the blurred lines between mortal and divine. Because they carried divine blood, they could influence the course of wars, slay monsters, or even ascend to godhood if they proved themselves worthy. Yet they also experienced human emotions—love, fear, anger—and could suffer painful consequences from the gods' conflicts.

6.8.2 Hero Cults in Greek Society

After their deaths, some heroes were worshipped at shrines, receiving **hero cults**. Locals believed these departed heroes could still protect their communities from beyond the grave. Heracles, for instance, was sometimes honored not just as a hero but as a god who rose to Olympus after his mortal life ended. These cults showed that heroic deeds left a lasting mark, bridging mortal limitations and divine reverence.

Hero cults also reinforced civic pride. A city might claim a famous hero as its founder or patron, hosting annual games or festivals in the hero's name. This practice blended religious devotion with local identity, strengthening the sense of community and shared mythological heritage.

6.9 Conflicts and Lessons in Mortal-God Relationships

6.9.1 Love and Betrayal

The Greek gods frequently fell in love with mortals. Stories of Zeus's many affairs are well-known, but other gods like Apollo and Poseidon also had relationships with humans. While some romances ended happily—with the mortal receiving gifts or a place in a god's heart—many ended tragically. For instance, Apollo's beloved **Hyacinthus** was accidentally killed by a discus throw, after which Apollo created the hyacinth flower in his memory.

Such tales explore the fragility of mortal life when touched by divine passion. Even well-intentioned gods could inadvertently cause heartbreak or death. The moral could be interpreted as a warning about the inherent imbalance in a mortal-god relationship. No matter how sincere the affection, the power gap often led to sorrow.

6.9.2 Moral Lessons

Greek myths do not always present gods as moral examples—some deities act out of envy or anger, ignoring justice. Instead, the stories emphasize that mortals must navigate these powerful personalities carefully. Showing respect through offerings, prayers, and humility could earn a god's protection. Displaying arrogance or challenging a god's domain would likely bring ruin.

Such teachings extended to everyday life: citizens were reminded to honor traditions, respect natural forces, and maintain social harmony. The gods could be unpredictable, so it was wise to avoid giving them a reason to unleash their wrath. At the same time, myths also provided hope: with the gods' favor, even a humble mortal could achieve great deeds.

6.10 Philosophical Interpretations

6.10.1 Changing Views in Later Periods

Over time, Greek thinkers like **Xenophanes**, **Plato**, and **Aristotle** questioned the literal truth of myths. They critiqued stories that depicted gods behaving immorally, suggesting these tales might be allegories or reflections of earlier poetic traditions. Some philosophers proposed a higher, more abstract deity or a set of natural principles behind the gods' actions.

Still, the cultural core remained: the idea that mortals inhabit a world shaped by divine forces, needing to show respect while striving to grow and learn. Even if the philosophers reinterpreted the myths, they acknowledged their educational and moral value within society.

6.10.2 Legacy of Mortal-God Interaction

These debates did not erase the myths; instead, they enriched the tradition. Myths continued to be told in plays, festivals, and art. The tension between mortal freedom and divine power became a central theme in Greek drama, especially tragedies by **Sophocles**, **Euripides**, and **Aeschylus**. Characters in these plays wrestled with fate, prophecy, and the will of the gods, reflecting the real-life anxieties and values of Greek audiences.

6.11 Conclusion of Chapter 6

The relationship between **mortals and the gods** lies at the heart of Greek mythology. From simple prayers to epic quests, from cautionary tales of hubris to inspiring stories of divine favor, these myths teach us about humility, perseverance, and respect. Mortals are not powerless—they can gain wisdom, defy obstacles, and even contend with gods—but they must be mindful of divine limits.

In reading about how mortals and gods interact, we see a reflection of universal human experiences: hope, fear, ambition, love, and the search for meaning. The gods, with all their might and flaws, become forces that mortals must negotiate with, adapting to the uncertain world around them.

CHAPTER 7

Heroes in Greek Mythology

7.1 Introduction: What Makes a Hero?

In ancient Greek mythology, **heroes** were mortals—or sometimes demi-gods—who performed remarkable feats. They fought monsters, traveled to distant lands, won wars, and occasionally challenged the gods themselves. These heroes were not perfect. They often had flaws such as pride, anger, or doubt. Yet, it was their courage, determination, and willingness to risk everything that set them apart.

The concept of a "hero" in Greek myth differs somewhat from modern ideas. These ancient figures did not always defend the weak or live by strict moral codes. Instead, they strove for **glory** (in Greek, *kleos*) and **honor** (*timē*). By performing near-impossible deeds, they gained fame that lasted even after death. At times, the gods helped them; at other times, the gods tested them harshly.

In this chapter, we will explore how heroes were viewed in ancient Greece, what qualities they embodied, and why their stories still resonate. Heroes remind us that ordinary humans—despite fears and mistakes—can achieve greatness. Their triumphs, tragedies, and lessons form a large part of Greek mythology, bridging the mortal world and the realm of the divine.

7.2 Origins of the Heroic Tradition

7.2.1 Semi-Divine Ancestry

Many Greek heroes were said to have a **divine parent**, typically one of the Olympians. For instance, **Heracles** (Roman name: Hercules) was the son of Zeus and a mortal woman named Alcmene. **Perseus** was also a son of Zeus, and **Theseus** often claimed lineage from Poseidon in some versions of the myth. This mix of godly power and mortal vulnerability made them unique—stronger or braver than ordinary people but still fated to die.

By having a god as a parent, these heroes inherited certain gifts. They might possess remarkable strength, extraordinary courage, or special protection in battle. However, they also inherited **enemies** among the gods. When one deity favored a hero, another might resent that hero, often out of jealousy or rivalry. This tension shaped the hero's path, creating trials far beyond normal human experiences.

7.2.2 Cultural Values and Mythic Storytelling

Heroes in Greek myth also arose from the **oral tradition**, where bards recited epic poems around fires or in marketplaces. Stories of great deeds captivated audiences and served as moral lessons or entertainment. The Greeks admired physical strength, cleverness, loyalty, and the willingness to **strive for honor**. Heroes showed these qualities, each in a unique way.

Yet, the heroic code also allowed for personal flaws like hubris—excessive pride. These flaws often drove the heroes into more incredible adventures or led to their downfall. The tension between a hero's gifts and faults made for dramatic storytelling, teaching listeners that success demands skill and virtue, but arrogance can undo even the strongest.

7.3 Common Traits of Greek Heroes

7.3.1 Courage and Determination

One trait all heroes share is the ability to face danger bravely. Heroes do not necessarily feel no fear; they simply act despite being afraid. Perseus faced the terrifying Medusa, whose gaze could turn people to stone, yet continued. Theseus descended into a dark labyrinth to confront the Minotaur. By displaying courage in the face of death or the unknown, Greek heroes earned everlasting renown.

Determination often accompanies courage. Heroes persist when a quest seems impossible, forging ahead even when obstacles mount. They rely on their wits, physical power, and sometimes divine guidance. Their willingness to keep going, no matter the cost, sets them apart from ordinary folk who might give up in despair.

7.3.2 Favor of the Gods (and Rivalries)

Many heroes receive direct help from a god or goddess who takes a liking to them. **Athena** is known for guiding clever heroes, while **Zeus** might protect a son he fathered. However, other deities might oppose these heroes with equal force. This divine tug-of-war influences the hero's journey, forcing them to win not just on a physical level but also within the complex politics of Olympus.

In some cases, a hero's success hinges on performing rituals correctly, showing gratitude through offerings, or honoring a specific deity. The slightest insult could turn a helpful god into a bitter enemy. Heroes thus had to be pious as well as brave, balancing boldness with reverence for the powerful beings above them.

7.4 The Heroic Cycle: From Call to Quest

7.4.1 The Call to Adventure

Many hero myths follow a **call to adventure**—an event that draws the hero out of normal life and into danger. This call might be a prophecy, a sudden crisis, or a challenge set by a king or a god. For Theseus, it was learning of the Minotaur's threat to Athens. For Jason, it was retrieving the **Golden Fleece** to claim his rightful throne. Such calls create a sense of **destiny**, suggesting the hero is meant for greatness.

Sometimes the hero hesitates. After all, the tasks set before them are daunting, often involving monsters, journeying to far-off lands, or standing against tyrants. Yet, if they refuse, misfortune might befall them or their families. Greek myths thus teach that ignoring one's destiny can lead to greater harm than facing it head-on.

7.4.2 Trials and Allies

Once the hero accepts the call, they undergo a series of **trials**. These can be physical ordeals—slaying a beast, wrestling a giant, sailing through perilous seas—or mental puzzles requiring strategy and cunning. Along the way, the hero meets allies: a wise elder, a helpful nymph, or even a minor god who has taken a liking to them. These friends provide guidance, magical items, or moral support.

At the center of most hero myths lies a significant challenge or climax—sometimes called the hero's "supreme ordeal." Overcoming it often involves a personal transformation. By learning humility, trusting friends, or outsmarting a foe, the hero grows. This personal development is as vital as the external victory. The Greeks valued **arete**—excellence in character—alongside arete in physical skill.

7.5 Major Greek Heroes and Their Stories

To illustrate these points, let us explore some of the most famous figures:

7.5.1 Perseus: The Gorgon-Slayer

Perseus was the son of Zeus and the mortal princess **Danaë**. Cast into the sea in a chest by his grandfather (who feared a prophecy that Perseus would be his doom), Perseus survived and grew into a strong youth. A scheming king later demanded an impossible gift: the head of **Medusa**—a monstrous Gorgon with snakes for hair. Anyone who looked into her eyes turned to stone.

- **Divine Help**: Perseus received gifts from several gods. **Athena** gave him a polished shield to view Medusa's reflection safely, **Hermes** provided winged sandals to fly, and he also gained a magic sword and a special pouch.

- **Trials**: Perseus traveled to the edge of the known world, seeking the **Graeae**—three old sisters sharing one eye and one tooth—who revealed Medusa's location. After beheading Medusa, he fled with her severed head, which still retained its petrifying power.
- **Return and Legacy**: On his way home, Perseus rescued **Andromeda** from a sea monster, later marrying her. Upon returning, he used Medusa's head to turn the wicked king to stone, freeing his mother. Eventually, Perseus's actions led to the fulfillment of the prophecy—his grandfather died in a tragic accident, confirming that fate cannot be escaped.

Perseus's story shows courage, cleverness, and reliance on divine tools. His victory over Medusa symbolized triumph over impossible odds, and his respect for the gods earned him success.

7.5.2 Theseus: The Labyrinth Conqueror

Theseus grew up without knowing his father, King Aegeus of Athens. When he learned of his royal blood, he set out to meet Aegeus, facing brigands and monsters along the way. He overcame each with cunning and strength, proving himself a hero even before reaching Athens.

- **Call to Adventure**: Athens was forced to send young men and women as tribute to Crete, where they would be devoured by the **Minotaur**, a half-man, half-bull beast within a labyrinth. Theseus volunteered to end this horror.
- **Trial in the Labyrinth**: With help from **Ariadne**, daughter of King Minos, Theseus used a ball of thread to track his path. He navigated the maze, slew the Minotaur, and escaped.
- **Tragic Return**: Though he succeeded, Theseus forgot to change the black sails on his ship to white ones, a prearranged signal of success. Seeing the black sails, King Aegeus believed his son dead and threw himself into the sea, hence the name "Aegean Sea."

Theseus's tale highlights intelligence and bravery but ends with personal sorrow. It underscores how even heroes can make fatal errors, bringing unintended tragedies.

7.5.3 Bellerophon: Rider of Pegasus

Bellerophon was known for taming the winged horse **Pegasus**. Some myths say Athena gave him a golden bridle in a dream, enabling him to catch Pegasus near a sacred spring. Riding Pegasus, Bellerophon performed heroic deeds such as slaying the **Chimera**, a fire-breathing monster with a lion's head, goat's body, and serpent's tail.

- **Hubris**: Buoyed by his success, Bellerophon grew proud. He tried to fly Pegasus to Mount Olympus, seeking a place among the gods.
- **Downfall**: Offended by this arrogance, Zeus sent a gadfly to sting Pegasus. The startled horse threw Bellerophon, who fell back to Earth. Crippled and blinded, Bellerophon wandered in misery, a cautionary tale about the danger of equating oneself with gods.

His story, like many others, warns that glory must be balanced by humility. No matter how heroic, mortals cannot force entry into Olympus.

7.6 Heroic Flaws and Lessons

Greek heroes often suffer from **tragic flaws**, reflecting a deeper moral dimension to their tales:

- **Pride (Hubris)**: As seen in Bellerophon's downfall.
- **Rashness**: Many heroes act before thinking, such as Theseus's oversight with the sails.
- **Wrath**: Some, like **Achilles**, struggle with anger that can cloud judgment and harm allies.

The Greek audience learned that heroism is not about perfection; it is about striving for excellence despite human weaknesses. A hero's success lies in balancing ambition with respect for divine laws and seeking wisdom alongside might.

7.7 Hero Cults and Honors

7.7.1 Shrines and Offerings

After death, heroes sometimes received **hero cults**, where people honored them at local shrines. Citizens believed these heroes could protect their land from invaders or natural disasters. They offered animals, wine, or small gifts to the hero's spirit. Such cults gave communities a sense of shared identity, pride, and spiritual connection.

For instance, the city of **Sparta** worshiped the hero **Menelaus**, who was central to the Trojan War. **Athens** honored Theseus as a founding father. These shrines were places of memory, teaching new generations about their city's mythical heritage and the values heroes stood for.

7.7.2 Festival Competitions

To celebrate heroes, city-states might hold **games** or **performances** in their honor. Athletic competitions, chariot races, or recitations of epic poetry reminded the crowd of past heroism and inspired present-day virtue. By linking local heroes to civic pride, these events kept the heroic tradition alive, knitting together the social fabric around shared legends.

7.8 The Evolving Idea of a Hero

Over centuries, Greek mythology evolved, influenced by poets like **Homer** and dramatists like **Sophocles** and **Euripides**. Early hero tales portrayed larger-than-life figures battling monsters and gods. Later works delved more into **moral questions**, showing heroes wrestling with guilt, destiny, and conflicting duties. For example, **Oedipus** becomes a tragic hero who unknowingly kills his father and marries his mother. His story, while lacking monster-slaying, reveals the tension between fate and free will, and the heroic decision to face truth rather than deny it.

This shift shows how Greek society used hero myths to explore deeper human themes. It was not enough to conquer beasts; the real test was understanding oneself and accepting responsibility, even when destiny seemed cruel. Heroes thus became mirrors, reflecting the hopes, fears, and ethical dilemmas of the people who told their stories.

7.9 Female Heroes and Heroines

Greek myth is often dominated by male heroes, but **female heroines** also appear, though less frequently. Some, like **Atalanta**, stood out for their skill in hunting, speed, or archery. Atalanta outran all her suitors, refusing to marry unless a man could beat her in a footrace. Eventually, a clever suitor used golden apples from Aphrodite to distract her. This marriage ended unhappily, but Atalanta's independence and prowess resonated with listeners.

Another notable figure is **Penelope**, wife of Odysseus. Though not a warrior, she is often hailed for her cleverness and loyalty, resisting numerous suitors for twenty years while Odysseus was away. Penelope's cunning in weaving and unweaving a burial shroud to delay remarriage stands as a testament to female wit in the face of male pressure.

These examples reveal that heroism was not limited to battlefield deeds. Resourcefulness, loyalty, and the ability to uphold personal or family honor could also earn a form of heroic respect.

7.10 Heroes as Cultural Icons

7.10.1 Role Models and Warnings

To the ancient Greeks, heroes were **role models**—showing young people how to be brave, cunning, or loyal. But they also served as **warnings** against overreaching. The stories taught that one must keep faith with the gods and remember the limitations of mortality. In a society where personal honor was paramount, these dual lessons—strive for glory, beware of pride—guided individual and community behavior.

7.10.2 Artistic Representations

Vase paintings, sculptures, and temple friezes often depicted heroic scenes. The fight of Heracles with the Nemean Lion or Theseus battling the Minotaur adorned pottery and public buildings. Viewers recognized these images immediately, connecting them to shared myths. This art was more than decoration—it was a visual reminder of the cultural identity and moral values of the community.

CHAPTER 8

The Trojan War

8.1 Introduction: A War of Gods and Men

The **Trojan War** stands as one of the central events in Greek mythology. It was a long, bitter conflict pitting the allied forces of **Achaean** (Greek) city-states against the wealthy city of **Troy**. The war lasted ten years—if not longer—and involved famous heroes such as **Achilles**, **Odysseus**, and **Ajax**. It also drew **Olympian gods** into the fray, with each deity choosing sides or interfering as they saw fit.

The Trojan War is best known from two epic poems: the **Iliad**, which focuses on the wrath of Achilles during a segment of the war, and the **Odyssey**, which follows Odysseus's return home afterward. Though these poems present only slices of the full conflict, later authors and storytellers expanded the tale. This mythic war reflects Greek values about honor, pride, fate, and the tragic costs of human ambition.

In this chapter, we will explore the causes of the war, key events and characters, how the gods influenced the battles, and the lasting legacy of Troy's downfall. The Trojan War is not just a story of sieges and sword fights—it is also a cautionary tale about desire, betrayal, loyalty, and the devastating power of **ego** when fueled by the gods.

8.2 The Seeds of Conflict: The Judgment of Paris

8.2.1 The Beauty Contest Among the Goddesses

The Trojan War's beginnings trace back to a **divine rivalry**. At a wedding feast of Peleus and Thetis (parents of Achilles), the goddess of discord, **Eris**, tossed a golden apple inscribed with the words "For the Fairest." **Hera**, **Athena**, and **Aphrodite** each claimed the apple. To settle who deserved it, Zeus assigned the judgment to **Paris**, a prince of Troy known for his fairness in judging beauty.

Paris found himself in a tricky spot. Each goddess offered him a bribe:

- **Hera** offered royal power over vast territories.
- **Athena** promised wisdom and victory in war.
- **Aphrodite** tempted him with the love of the most beautiful woman in the world.

Swayed by desire, Paris awarded the apple to Aphrodite, effectively earning Hera and Athena's anger. Aphrodite kept her promise, but there was a catch—the most beautiful woman, **Helen**, was already married to King Menelaus of Sparta.

8.2.2 Abduction of Helen

Aphrodite led Paris to Sparta, where he met Helen. Whether Helen left willingly or was seduced by Aphrodite's magic is debated in myth, but the result was the same: Paris took Helen away to Troy, making her "Helen of Troy." Outraged, Menelaus called upon his brother, **Agamemnon**, King of Mycenae, and other Greek kings to help retrieve Helen. They assembled a massive fleet and sailed to Troy, igniting the war.

This chain of events demonstrates the **interwoven actions of gods and mortals**. A divine beauty contest triggered a mortal kidnapping, leading to a decade of bloodshed. Pride and lust took precedence over wisdom, and the outcome would shape legends for centuries.

8.3 The Assembled Greek Forces

8.3.1 Famous Kings and Warriors

To rescue Helen, the Greek kings and heroes formed a coalition often called the "Achaean" force. Key figures included:

- **Agamemnon**: High King and leader of the expedition; brother of Menelaus.
- **Menelaus**: Helen's husband, King of Sparta, whose honor was at stake.
- **Odysseus**: King of Ithaca, known for his clever mind.
- **Ajax the Great**: A colossal warrior famed for his strength.

- **Diomedes**: A skilled fighter with close ties to the goddess Athena.
- **Nestor**: King of Pylos, an old and wise counselor.
- **Achilles**: The greatest Greek warrior, son of Peleus and the sea-nymph Thetis.

Each brought their own armies, ships, and personal motivations—some sought glory, others treasure, and a few hoped to stay in the gods' favor by avenging Menelaus's loss.

8.3.2 The Wrath of Achilles

Before the war commenced, an important prophecy stated that the Greeks could not take Troy without Achilles. But Achilles himself was not easy to command. A proud and temperamental warrior, Achilles brought not just unmatched skill but also a fatal flaw—**anger**. His mother, Thetis, tried to protect him by dipping him in the River Styx as a baby, rendering him nearly invulnerable except for his **heel**, where she held him.

This detail of the "Achilles' heel" would later symbolize a hidden vulnerability. From the start, Achilles's presence loomed over the war like a storm cloud, both indispensable and unpredictable.

8.4 The Walls of Troy and Its Defenders

8.4.1 Mighty Troy

Troy was no ordinary city. Its walls were said to have been built with divine assistance, making them nearly impossible to breach. The city grew wealthy from trade, commanding strategic points near the Dardanelles strait. King **Priam** ruled with wisdom, fathering many children, including **Hector** and **Paris**.

- **Hector**: Troy's greatest champion, beloved by his people. He was a courageous and honorable warrior.
- **Paris**: Not as skilled in combat as Hector, but fated to play a crucial role in the war due to his involvement with Helen.

Despite the moral ambiguity of the kidnapping, the Trojans were defending their homeland. They believed in protecting their prince, and Troy's high walls offered confidence that they could outlast the Greek siege.

8.4.2 Allied Trojans

Various allies joined Troy, including contingents from nearby regions such as Lycia. Notable ally warriors like **Sarpedon** fought valiantly on Troy's side, often urged by the gods who supported them—especially **Aphrodite** and **Apollo**. These forces contributed might and morale, making the Trojan side formidable.

8.5 The Gods Take Sides

8.5.1 Divine Alliances

The Trojan War saw a pantheon split by the **Judgment of Paris**.

- **Hera** and **Athena**, enraged by Paris's choice, supported the Greeks.
- **Aphrodite**, who won the beauty contest, backed Troy to protect Paris.
- **Apollo** also leaned toward Troy, sometimes because of personal grudges against the Greeks or favoritism toward Trojan heroes.
- **Zeus**, in theory, attempted neutrality but often leaned one way or another to maintain balance or fulfill fate.

This divine involvement turned the battlefield into a cosmic stage. A Greek warrior might find success with Athena's guidance, only to be thwarted when Apollo intervened. Even so, there were limits: the gods generally avoided direct kills of major heroes, preferring to nudge events rather than openly break fate's decrees.

8.5.2 Fated Outcomes

Zeus possessed scales of fate, which he could tip slightly but never overturn entirely. From the start, it was said that Troy would eventually fall. Yet the war's exact path—who would die, how the city would be taken—remained uncertain. This interplay of **fate** and **free will** enthralled ancient audiences, showing that even gods could not fully escape destiny's hold.

8.6 Key Episodes in the War

8.6.1 Early Battles and Stalemates

When the Greeks arrived on Trojan shores, initial skirmishes proved inconclusive. The Trojans defended behind their walls. The Greeks established a beachhead camp, raiding nearby lands for resources. Occasional duels took place, like a face-off between **Menelaus** and **Paris** that ended indecisively when Aphrodite whisked Paris away in a cloud.

This period showed the war's **stalemate** nature. Despite the famed Greek heroes and Troy's resolute defenders, neither side could achieve a swift victory. The conflict dragged on, straining morale and resources. Some Trojans urged returning Helen to avoid devastation, but King Priam and Prince Paris refused.

8.6.2 The Quarrel Between Agamemnon and Achilles

A pivotal dispute erupted when **Agamemnon** claimed a war prize (a captive woman named Briseis) that Achilles considered rightfully his.

Feeling dishonored, Achilles **withdrew** from the fighting, refusing to lead his men. This event, captured in Homer's **Iliad**, caused Greek fortunes to plummet. Without Achilles, their best warrior, the Trojans, led by Hector, drove the Greeks closer to their ships.

This episode highlights the destructive power of **personal pride** in a collective effort. Achilles's wrath overshadowed strategy, putting all Greek warriors at risk. Agamemnon, equally prideful, refused to yield. The war became as much a clash of egos as a military campaign.

8.6.3 Hector's Bravery and Tragic Fate

During Achilles's absence, **Hector** dominated the battlefield. He was more than a skilled warrior—he was a devoted family man, husband to **Andromache**, father to a young son. The Trojans viewed him as their beacon of hope. Yet fate had other plans.

- **Patroclus's Death**: Achilles's close friend, **Patroclus**, borrowed his armor to rally the Greeks. Hector, mistaking Patroclus for Achilles, killed him. This act forced Achilles back into the fight, fueled by overwhelming grief and rage.
- **Achilles vs. Hector**: When Achilles returned, he sought vengeance. Hector, though valiant, could not match Achilles's divine-touched might. Their duel ended with Hector's death, an event that spelled doom for Troy. Achilles desecrated Hector's body out of fury, dragging it behind his chariot. Only King Priam's brave plea, humbling himself before Achilles, secured Hector's proper funeral.

Hector's fall and Achilles's harsh revenge exemplify how **rage blinds even the greatest warrior** to moral considerations. Hector died a hero, Achilles lived as a killer in the moment, forging a bleak contrast between noble duty and uncontrolled fury.

8.7 The Fall of Achilles and the Trojan Horse

8.7.1 Achilles's Heel

Achilles continued to fight, unstoppable. But his divine partial invulnerability did not guarantee immortality. The Trojan prince **Paris**, aided by Apollo, shot an arrow that struck Achilles's only weak spot—his **heel**. Achilles fell. The greatest Greek warrior died not in a grand battle of equals, but from a single well-placed arrow, showing how even the mightiest hero remains mortal.

His death shocked the Greek forces, yet the war continued. Achilles's armor was awarded to **Odysseus**, angering **Ajax**, who believed he deserved it. Ajax eventually took his own life in despair, one more tragic casualty of the war's destructive nature.

8.7.2 Odysseus's Cunning and the Trojan Horse

Realizing brute force would never breach Troy's walls, Odysseus devised a **ruse**—the famous **Trojan Horse**. The Greeks built a massive wooden horse, hid warriors inside it, and pretended to sail away, leaving the horse as an offering to the gods. The Trojans, despite warnings from prophets like **Cassandra**, brought the horse within their gates to celebrate the "end" of the siege.

That night, the hidden Greeks slipped out, opened the gates for the returning army, and unleashed havoc. Troy burned. King Priam was slain, the Trojan men were killed or enslaved, and Helen was reunited with Menelaus. This cunning trick sealed Troy's fate, marking a bitter triumph for the Greeks.

8.8 Aftermath and Moral Reflections

8.8.1 The Greeks' Difficult Return

Though victorious, many Greeks suffered on their journey home, facing storms and curses from the gods who found their actions cruel. The destruction of Troy did not yield unbridled joy; it revealed the **harsh cost** of war. For example:

- **Agamemnon** returned to a tragic fate, murdered by his wife Clytemnestra in revenge for sacrificing their daughter before the war.
- **Menelaus** and Helen wandered before reestablishing their rule in Sparta.
- **Odysseus** took ten more years to reach Ithaca, as told in the **Odyssey**.

These tales show how victory can be **hollow** if achieved through deceit or excessive brutality. Gods who once aided the Greeks turned against them, illustrating that alignment with the divine is fragile and often based on ethical conduct.

8.8.2 Survivors and Founding Legends

Survivors on the Trojan side also feature in later stories. **Aeneas**, a Trojan prince, escaped the city's fall and journeyed west, eventually leading to legends of the founding of Rome. Though that tradition is more Roman than Greek, it connects the Trojan War's end to a broader Mediterranean narrative.

For the Greeks themselves, the war became a rich source of **myth, literature, and drama**. Poets like Homer, playwrights like Euripides, and countless storytellers retold the events, emphasizing the war's lessons on the interplay of love, pride, fate, and the gods.

8.9 Role of the Trojan War in Greek Culture

8.9.1 Epic Poetry and Identity

The **Iliad** and **Odyssey**, attributed to **Homer**, were cornerstones of Greek education. Children memorized lines from these epics, absorbing the heroic ideals of courage, loyalty, and cunning. Soldiers looked to Achilles as the model of valor, though also cautioning themselves against his uncontrolled anger. Odysseus's intelligence showed that might alone was not enough. These epics shaped Greek identity, making the Trojan War almost a **historical** event in public memory, even though its mythic elements are clear.

8.9.2 Religious and Moral Undertones

Like many Greek myths, the Trojan War taught about **piety** and **moderation**. The gods punished arrogance—Paris's judgment offended Hera and Athena, Achilles's disrespect for Hector's body angered the gods, and the Greeks' merciless sacking of Troy brought them curses. By weaving divine retribution into the narrative, the myths reinforced the Greek belief that mortals must never forget their place.

Additionally, the war revealed how desire can escalate into chaos, from Paris's lust for Helen to Agamemnon's thirst for power. This moral dimension warned Greeks to guard their impulses, or risk repeating Troy's fate.

8.10 The Trojan War's Enduring Lessons

8.10.1 The Cost of Pride and Passion

Over and over, the Trojan War emphasizes that **pride**—whether in the form of personal glory or national honor—can spark terrible suffering. Paris's abduction of Helen might have seemed a romantic gesture, but it was ultimately reckless. Agamemnon's quarrel with Achilles placed individual pride above collective good, leading to near defeat. Even the war's final victory hinged on deception, suggesting that brute force alone fails when confronting strong defenses.

8.10.2 Heroes in War

The war also tested the concept of **heroism**. Figures like Achilles showed that physical excellence can win many battles but fails to conquer one's own rage or mortality. Heroes such as Hector displayed moral courage, defending family and city. Odysseus used cunning rather than unstoppable might. In each case, the story suggests multiple approaches to heroism—valor, wisdom, loyalty—but also reveals how war magnifies both virtues and vices.

8.11 Modern Echoes

Although we are avoiding direct references to modern times, it is clear that the story of the Trojan War continued to influence later cultures in the ancient world. Historians, poets, and dramatists all used these myths to reflect on **human nature**—how quickly conflicts can escalate, how an entire generation can be swept into violence, and how the winners often suffer nearly as much as the losers.

In the Greek tradition, the Trojan War stands as the ultimate example of a conflict ignited by **love** and **anger** but fueled by countless personal ambitions, misunderstandings, and divine meddling. It remains a major lens through which ancient Greeks examined themes like fate, sacrifice, and the cost of greatness.

CHAPTER 9

Odysseus and His Journey

9.1 Introduction: The Cunning Hero

Few Greek heroes are as famous for their **wit** and **endurance** as **Odysseus**, King of Ithaca. While many heroes are known for physical strength—Achilles, Hercules, Theseus—Odysseus stands out for his **cunning** mind. He led the Greek forces to victory in the Trojan War through strategy (most notably the Trojan Horse) and later embarked on a long and perilous voyage home, told in Homer's **Odyssey**.

This journey tested not only his survival skills, but also his loyalty, patience, and humility. For ten years, Odysseus roamed from island to island, encountering enchantresses, monsters, and the wrath of gods, especially **Poseidon**. His story reveals the importance of perseverance, the power of intelligence, and the complex relationship mortals share with gods who can both help and hinder them.

9.2 Background: The End of the Trojan War

9.2.1 Leaving Troy

After ten years of siege, the Trojan War ended with Odysseus's Trojan Horse ruse. The Greek armies sacked the city of Troy, claiming victory. Many warriors returned home quickly, but Odysseus's fate was different. He had angered **Poseidon** by blinding the Cyclops Polyphemus (Poseidon's son), setting off a chain of curses that made his voyage treacherous.

Odysseus sailed from Troy with twelve ships, manned by loyal Ithacan companions. They expected a relatively swift trip back to Ithaca, an island off western Greece. Yet the storms that soon battered their fleet were no ordinary events. They revealed the **wrath of gods** who were determined to prolong Odysseus's suffering, testing his character at every turn.

9.2.2 The Prophecy of Tiresias

Before leaving, Odysseus learned from the prophet **Tiresias** that his journey would be difficult. He was told to avoid harming certain sacred animals belonging to the sun god Helios and to rely on cunning and patience rather than sheer force. Tiresias's warning highlighted the fine line Odysseus would walk—honor the gods' wishes, or face their fury. Even with forewarning, mortal desires and missteps often steered Odysseus into danger.

9.3 First Trials: The Cicones and the Lotus-Eaters

9.3.1 The Raid on the Cicones

Shortly after sailing away from Troy, Odysseus and his men attacked the land of the **Cicones**, plundering its riches. However, the Cicones soon rallied reinforcement, driving the Greeks back and killing several of Odysseus's men. This early setback showed the danger of **greed** and **overconfidence**. Instead of sailing home promptly, they lingered to gather loot, paying a costly price.

9.3.2 The Lotus-Eaters

Continuing their voyage, Odysseus's fleet was blown off course to a strange shore inhabited by the **Lotus-Eaters**, a people who consumed the lotus plant that caused blissful forgetfulness. Several of Odysseus's men ate the lotus, losing all desire to return home. Only by force did Odysseus drag them back to the ships, showing his **leadership** in resisting temptation. This episode highlights how losing sight of one's goals—lured by pleasure—can sabotage even the bravest individuals.

9.4 The Cyclops: A Deadly Encounter

9.4.1 Polyphemus's Cave

Odysseus's next major challenge was the Cyclops **Polyphemus**, a gigantic one-eyed shepherd. Odysseus and his men, seeking shelter and provisions, entered Polyphemus's cave uninvited. When the Cyclops returned, he sealed the cave's entrance with a massive boulder and began devouring Odysseus's men. Faced with certain doom, Odysseus devised a plan:

1. **Trickery**: He told Polyphemus his name was "Nobody."
2. **Wine**: He offered the Cyclops strong wine to make him drowsy.
3. **Blinding**: While Polyphemus slept, Odysseus and his men heated a sharpened stake in the fire and blinded his single eye.

9.4.2 The Escape and Curse

Once Polyphemus was blinded, he rolled away the boulder to call for help from other Cyclopes. But when they asked who hurt him, he answered "Nobody!"—leading them to believe no one harmed him. Odysseus and his crew escaped by clinging to the undersides of Polyphemus's sheep, slipping out unseen.

However, Odysseus made a **grave mistake** as he sailed away: he taunted Polyphemus, revealing his true name. In fury, Polyphemus prayed to his father, Poseidon, to curse Odysseus. Thus began the **god of the sea**'s relentless pursuit of vengeance, ensuring Odysseus's journey would be fraught with storms and delays.

9.5 Aeolus, the Laestrygonians, and Circe

9.5.1 Aeolus and the Bag of Winds

Odysseus next found refuge with **Aeolus**, the keeper of the winds. Aeolus, impressed by Odysseus's story, gifted him a **bag containing all winds** except the gentle west wind that would carry them home. Odysseus cautioned his men not to open it. Yet, just as Ithaca's shores came into sight, curiosity and suspicion plagued his crew. They feared the bag held treasures Odysseus withheld from them, so they opened it, releasing the winds in a raging storm that blew them far from home again.

This episode underscores how **lack of trust and discipline** within a group can destroy progress. Odysseus's men, doubting their leader, unravelled Aeolus's gift, pushing Ithaca out of reach once more.

9.5.2 The Laestrygonians: Cannibal Giants

Next, the fleet landed among the **Laestrygonians**, a tribe of giant cannibals. Odysseus's scouts were attacked, and only Odysseus's ship escaped. The others were destroyed, devoured along with their crews. This catastrophic loss left Odysseus with a single ship, reinforcing the theme that prideful or careless exploration could be fatal in unknown lands. Here, as before, cunning and quick thinking saved Odysseus from total annihilation.

9.5.3 Circe's Island

Odysseus then reached the island of **Aeaea**, home to the sorceress **Circe**. She lured some of his men into her palace with enchanting food and drink, transforming them into swine. Forewarned by a divine messenger—often said to be **Hermes**—Odysseus consumed a protective herb called **moly**, resisting Circe's magic. Armed with this defense, he forced Circe to free his men.

Circe, seeing Odysseus's resilience, became a **hostess and ally**, offering shelter for a year. She also provided crucial advice: to continue home, Odysseus must journey to the **Underworld** and consult the prophet Tiresias for guidance. This turning point revealed a gentler side of Circe, showing how a formidable threat could become an ally when faced with Odysseus's courage and respect.

9.6 Journey to the Underworld

9.6.1 Seeking Tiresias

Following Circe's directions, Odysseus sailed to the land of the **Cimmerians**, a misty, gloomy place at the edge of the world. There, he performed **ritual offerings** to summon the dead. The ghost of **Tiresias** emerged, warning him again of the **Sun God's cattle** on the island of Thrinacia—if his men harmed them, they would be doomed. Tiresias also prophesied Odysseus's eventual return to Ithaca but hinted at further trials, including the possibility of more journeys even after regaining his throne.

9.6.2 Encounters with the Departed

In this Underworld visit, Odysseus spoke with the spirits of **his mother** (whom he had not known had died), **Agamemnon**, and **Achilles**, among others. Aching for their lost lives, these spirits offered bleak reflections on mortality, heroism, and regret. Achilles famously declared he would rather be a living servant than a lord among the dead, underscoring Greek beliefs that the Underworld was a sorrowful existence.

These encounters heightened Odysseus's **resolve** to return home, cherishing life among the living, no matter how hard the journey.

9.7 The Sirens, Scylla, and Charybdis

9.7.1 Resisting the Sirens

After returning to Circe's island briefly for final guidance, Odysseus set sail. Circe warned of the **Sirens**, creatures whose irresistible song lured sailors to their deaths on rocky shores. Odysseus ordered his men to plug their ears with wax and instructed them to tie him tightly to the mast so he alone could hear the Sirens' song but not act on it.

This tactic succeeded. Though Odysseus strained at his bonds, longing to go to the Sirens, his men kept rowing until they were safely past. This episode symbolizes the victory of **forethought and planning** over deadly temptation.

9.7.2 The Monsters: Scylla and Charybdis

Further ahead lay two infamous perils:

- **Scylla**: A six-headed monster perched on a cliff, snatching sailors from passing ships.
- **Charybdis**: A vast whirlpool that sucked down entire vessels, drowning them in swirling waters.

Following Circe's counsel, Odysseus chose to sail closer to Scylla, losing six men rather than risking his entire ship to Charybdis. The terror of these sea monsters reflected the **unavoidable costs** of certain choices. Sometimes, even cunning leaders must pick the lesser of two evils, accepting losses to save the majority.

9.8 The Sun God's Cattle and the Final Wrath of Zeus

9.8.1 Thrinacia: The Forbidden Herds

Odysseus's crew next landed on **Thrinacia**, the island where the Sun God **Helios** kept his sacred cattle. Warned by Tiresias and Circe, Odysseus forbade anyone to harm these animals. Yet strong winds trapped them on the island, and their food supplies dwindled. One day, while Odysseus slept, the desperate crew slaughtered some of Helios's cattle for sustenance.

9.8.2 Zeus's Punishment

Enraged, Helios threatened to **withdraw the sun** from the world if justice was not served. Zeus responded by smashing Odysseus's ship with a thunderbolt when they finally left Thrinacia, killing all crew members. Only Odysseus survived, clinging to debris. This **divine punishment** emphasized the absolute power of gods and the dire consequences of **disobedience** to prophecy.

9.9 Calypso's Island and the Phaeacians

9.9.1 Captivity with Calypso

Adrift at sea, Odysseus washed up on the island of **Ogygia**, home to the nymph **Calypso**. She sheltered him, and over time, fell in love. Calypso offered Odysseus **immortality** if he stayed as her husband. Yet Odysseus yearned for Ithaca and his wife, **Penelope**. For seven years, he remained captive, longing to return home. The goddess Athena eventually intervened, appealing to Zeus, who sent **Hermes** to command Calypso to let Odysseus go.

9.9.2 Shipwreck and the Phaeacians

Calypso reluctantly allowed Odysseus to build a raft and depart. On the open sea, Poseidon spotted him, unleashing another tempest. Odysseus was again shipwrecked, washing ashore on the land of the **Phaeacians**. These hospitable people, ruled by King Alcinous and Queen Arete, welcomed Odysseus, who recounted his long tale of wanderings. Touched by his suffering, the Phaeacians gave him a ship to sail home.

9.10 Return to Ithaca and Vengeance

9.10.1 Penelope's Dilemma

During Odysseus's twenty-year absence (ten years at war, ten trying to return), Ithaca believed him dead. Many **suitors** vied for Penelope's hand, consuming Odysseus's wealth. Penelope, ever faithful, delayed them by weaving and unweaving a funeral shroud, claiming she would remarry only once it was complete. Each night, she secretly unraveled her day's work, stalling for years.

9.10.2 Odysseus's Disguise and the Bow Contest

Returning at last, Odysseus arrived in disguise, aided by Athena, to observe the situation. He discovered the suitors plotting to kill his son, **Telemachus**, and steal the throne. Penelope, nearly forced to choose a husband, announced a contest: whoever could string Odysseus's mighty bow and shoot an arrow through twelve axe heads would win her hand.

None of the suitors succeeded, but the disguised Odysseus did so effortlessly. Revealing his identity, he—alongside Telemachus—slaughtered the suitors. This violent retribution reclaimed his household, cleansing Ithaca of those who had betrayed his memory and harassed his wife. Though brutal, it was seen in Greek myth as **restoring justice** to the rightful king.

9.10.3 Reuniting with Penelope

Penelope, cautious after so many years of deception, tested Odysseus by mentioning their bed, which was built around a living olive tree. Only the real Odysseus would know its secrets. When he reacted passionately to her reference, Penelope recognized his identity. Their reunion symbolized not only the end of his journey but the triumph of **marital devotion** over time, distance, and adversity.

9.11 Themes and Lessons from Odysseus's Journey

9.11.1 Endurance and Loyalty

Odysseus's adventures show how **endurance** is crucial for survival. Storms, monsters, and divine obstacles tested every aspect of his character. Also, the loyalty between Odysseus and Penelope held firm despite temptations and uncertainties. Their faithfulness contrasted with the crew's frequent lapses, reminding audiences that personal dedication can overcome or endure divine hostility.

9.11.2 Intelligence Over Might

While Odysseus was capable in battle, his **cunning** was more valuable. From escaping Polyphemus to resisting the Sirens and masterminding the Trojan Horse, his intellect made him stand out among Greek heroes. This focus on strategy rather than brute force influenced how the Greeks viewed wisdom—an essential trait in leadership and survival. It also showed the importance of counsel from gods or wise figures, such as Athena or Tiresias.

9.11.3 Respect for the Divine and Mortal Boundaries

Revering the gods' warnings, fulfilling promises, and controlling impulses were keys to success. Where Odysseus honored these boundaries—like resisting the Sirens—he advanced. Where his men broke them—eating Helios's cattle—they faced disaster. In a broader sense, the Odyssey teaches that humans exist in a delicate balance with the supernatural world. Disregarding the gods' rules leads to peril, while respecting them can secure eventual triumph.

9.12 The Odyssey's Cultural Impact

9.12.1 Oral Epic Tradition

The **Odyssey**, along with the **Iliad**, formed the core of Greek epic poetry. Poets known as **rhapsodes** recited its verses in public gatherings, temples, and courts, shaping Greek education and cultural identity. Children learned these epics to understand bravery, humility, and devotion. The adventures of Odysseus echoed in countless plays and stories, highlighting a broad spectrum of human experiences—war, loss, love, growth, and redemption.

9.12.2 Odysseus as a Complex Hero

Odysseus stands apart because he embodies both **heroic valor** and **mortal frailty**. He is not invincible like Achilles in battle, nor purely righteous like some moral paragons. Instead, he is flawed—he lies, deceives, and occasionally yields to temptations. Yet his ultimate commitment to home and family redeems him in the eyes of the Greeks, illustrating that even cunning men can find a deeper loyalty that steadies them.

9.13 Conclusion of Chapter 9

Odysseus's journey home from Troy demonstrates the eternal struggle between mortal aspiration and divine influence. Despite repeated setbacks, he clings to the hope of returning to Ithaca and reuniting with his family. The epic's message is clear: **intelligence, perseverance, and faith** can guide one through unimaginable trials. Yet, success hinges on respecting divine boundaries and maintaining personal integrity in the face of relentless challenges.

From the siren calls of enchantresses to the horrors of sea monsters, the Odyssey's rich tapestry continues to fascinate. It reflects the Greek belief that life's journey often demands we navigate between reason and desire, humility and boldness, while trusting in the possibility of **homecoming** and reconciliation. In the next chapter, we will explore a different kind of hero, **Perseus**, whose feats revolve around slaying monstrous beings like Medusa. Each hero's story adds another dimension to the wide-ranging lessons of Greek mythology.

CHAPTER 10

Perseus and the Gorgons

10.1 Introduction: The Hero Destined to Slay Medusa

Perseus is one of the earliest known heroes in Greek mythology. The son of **Zeus** and the mortal **Danaë**, he rose to fame by defeating monstrous adversaries, most famously the Gorgon **Medusa**—a creature whose gaze could turn onlookers to stone. Perseus's saga involves prophecy, divine gifts, and cunning. He stands as an example of how unwavering courage, plus the gods' favor, can help mortals overcome terrifying supernatural threats.

Yet Perseus's life is also defined by the attempt to **escape fate**—his grandfather tried to prevent a prophecy that his grandson would cause his death, only to inadvertently set that destiny in motion. In exploring Perseus's adventures, we see themes of **family conflict**, **divine intervention**, and the blurred lines between monstrous and human realms.

10.2 Early Life: The Prophecy and Exile

10.2.1 Danaë's Imprisonment

Perseus's story begins with a **prophecy** given to King **Acrisius** of Argos. An oracle warned that Acrisius would be killed by his grandson. Terrified, Acrisius locked his only daughter, **Danaë**, in a bronze chamber to ensure she never bore children. However, **Zeus** took notice of Danaë's beauty and visited her in the form of golden rain, resulting in Perseus's conception.

When Acrisius discovered the baby, he feared the prophecy but hesitated to commit outright murder of his kin. Instead, he placed Danaë and the infant Perseus in a wooden chest, casting them into the sea, hoping fate or the gods would decide their survival.

10.2.2 Rescued by Dictys

The chest drifted to the island of **Seriphos**, where a fisherman named **Dictys** found and rescued them. Dictys welcomed Danaë and

Perseus into his home, raising Perseus to adulthood. Here, Perseus learned the values of **honor** and **humility**—yet his royal lineage and divine parentage would soon lead him into heroic deeds far beyond Seriphos's calm shores.

10.3 Polydectes's Challenge: The Quest for Medusa's Head

10.3.1 The King's Scheme

Dictys's brother, **Polydectes**, reigned as King of Seriphos. He lusted after Danaë, but Perseus protected his mother. To rid himself of Perseus, Polydectes pretended he desired the head of the **Gorgon Medusa** as a bridal gift—a monstrous request he believed Perseus could never fulfill. Feeling compelled to prove his worth, Perseus **vowed** to bring back Medusa's head, not realizing the deadly nature of his pledge.

10.3.2 Who Were the Gorgons?

Medusa was one of three Gorgons—winged sisters with snakes for hair. Unlike her immortal siblings, **Stheno** and **Euryale**, Medusa was **mortal**. A single glance at her face could turn any living creature to stone. Various myths explain Medusa's monstrous condition; one version suggests she was cursed by Athena for desecrating her temple. Regardless of how she gained her terrible power, Medusa dwelt in a remote lair, rarely seen by mortals.

Polydectes's challenge put Perseus in a near-impossible position: if he faced Medusa unprepared, he would become yet another statue in her dreadful collection.

10.4 Divine Assistance: Gifts from the Gods

10.4.1 Athena and Hermes

Before Perseus could embark, he received crucial support from two Olympians:

- **Athena**: The goddess of wisdom, outraged by Medusa's existence, sought the monster's destruction. She presented Perseus with a **polished bronze shield** that could act as a mirror, allowing him to view Medusa's reflection instead of her direct gaze.
- **Hermes**: The messenger god, often helpful to clever mortals, lent Perseus an **adamantine sword** (or a sickle in some versions) capable of decapitating the Gorgon. Hermes also guided Perseus in locating other items he would need, further demonstrating the gods' involvement in heroic quests.

10.4.2 The Graeae and the Cap of Invisibility

Following Athena's directions, Perseus went in search of the **Graeae**, three ancient sisters who shared a single eye and tooth. Only by seizing their eye mid-transfer could Perseus force them to reveal Medusa's location and the whereabouts of additional magical items:

- **Winged Sandals** of Hermes (or sometimes from the nymphs): granting flight.
- **Kibisis**: A special pouch to safely carry Medusa's head.
- **Cap of Invisibility** (belonging to Hades): allowing Perseus to hide from sight.

Armed with these artifacts, Perseus gained a fighting chance against the deadly Gorgon.

10.5 The Confrontation with Medusa

10.5.1 Approaching the Lair

Medusa's lair lay in a desolate region at the edge of the world. Statues of unfortunate victims littered the area—former warriors, beasts, or wanderers turned to stone. Perseus, guided by Athena's voice, moved carefully, wearing the Cap of Invisibility to hide from Medusa's gaze.

Using the **reflection** in Athena's shield, Perseus located Medusa without looking directly at her. This tactic required unwavering concentration, as even a momentary glance in the wrong direction meant instant petrification.

10.5.2 Striking the Mortal Blow

In a swift, precise motion, Perseus **beheaded** Medusa with Hermes's sword. From her blood sprang two offspring: the winged horse **Pegasus** and the giant **Chrysaor**. The other Gorgon sisters awoke, wailing at Medusa's death, but Perseus, still invisible, escaped swiftly on Hermes's sandals, placing Medusa's severed head in the kibisis.

This victory stands out in Greek myth for its **blend of intellect and bravery**. Perseus overcame an impossible challenge not through raw strength alone, but through divine gifts, cunning strategy, and calm execution under pressure.

10.6 Andromeda: The Princess in Distress

10.6.1 Saving Andromeda from the Sea Monster

On his journey back, Perseus passed through Ethiopia, where he found a princess named **Andromeda** chained to a rock by the sea. Her parents, King Cepheus and Queen Cassiopeia, had offended

Poseidon by boasting that Cassiopeia's beauty surpassed that of the sea nymphs. As punishment, Poseidon sent a sea monster to ravage their land. The oracle declared only sacrificing Andromeda could appease the deity.

Moved by her plight, Perseus confronted the sea monster. Some versions say he used **Medusa's head** to turn it to stone; others describe him fighting heroically with sword or spear. Either way, he rescued Andromeda. Grateful Cepheus offered his daughter's hand in marriage. Their union signaled Perseus's transformation from a wandering hero to a defender of the innocent, paralleling earlier epic champions who saved kingdoms from beasts.

10.6.2 Confrontation at the Wedding Feast

Andromeda was already betrothed to her uncle **Phineus**, who violently protested Perseus's claim. At the wedding banquet, a brawl broke out. Perseus, outnumbered, resorted to **Medusa's head** once more. He revealed it, turning Phineus and his allies to stone. This dramatic moment emphasized the Gorgon's power as both a blessing and a curse. Perseus's morality is questioned here—he fought for a just cause, yet the merciless petrification was a lethal solution, reflecting the sometimes harsh justice in Greek myths.

10.7 Return to Seriphos and Retribution

10.7.1 Punishing Polydectes

Having won glory abroad, Perseus at last returned to Seriphos. He discovered that Polydectes still harassed Danaë. In one version, Polydectes attempted to force Danaë into marriage, or claimed that Perseus's quest was a failure. Once again, Perseus wielded **Medusa's head** to turn Polydectes and his court to stone, freeing his mother. Dictys, the kind fisherman, became the new king of Seriphos, ensuring a just ruler took the throne.

10.7.2 Returning the Divine Tools

After these events, Perseus dutifully returned the magical artifacts to their rightful owners:

- The Cap of Invisibility back to Hades (or sometimes to Hermes).
- The Winged Sandals to Hermes.
- The shield to Athena.

He also offered **Medusa's head** to Athena, who placed it on her **Aegis** (shield or breastplate) as a symbol of protection and terror. This gesture underlined the respect Perseus had for the gods, acknowledging that his success came from their support as much as his own skill.

10.8 The Prophecy Fulfilled: Acrisius's Death

10.8.1 An Accidental Tragedy

Despite his victories, Perseus could not escape the prophecy concerning his grandfather, King Acrisius. Various versions recount how Perseus traveled to Argos, hoping for a reconciliation. Yet Acrisius fled, still fearing the prophecy. During an athletic contest—discus-throwing—Perseus's discus veered off and struck Acrisius, **killing him** instantly.

This event completed the tragic cycle: in trying to avoid the prophecy, Acrisius had set the course for it to happen. Perseus, though sorrowful, accepted fate's decree. In some tellings, he refused to rule Argos due to guilt, swapping kingdoms with another ruler and becoming king of **Tiryns** or founding **Mycenae**. This moral lesson is clear: humans cannot outmaneuver destiny, especially one shaped by the gods.

10.8.2 Legacy of Perseus

Perseus's line would eventually include **Heracles** (Hercules), among other noteworthy descendants. Thus, Perseus became an ancestor to some of Greece's greatest heroes. His story formed part of the genealogical and mythical foundation that city-states used to trace their origins to divine or heroic bloodlines, reinforcing civic pride and religious significance.

10.9 Themes in Perseus's Tale

10.9.1 Courage, Cunning, and Divine Aid

Perseus's defeat of Medusa highlights **courage** balanced with **intellect**. Like Odysseus, Perseus thrived by using strategy—reflective shields and stealth rather than direct confrontation. The unwavering presence of divine guidance, from Athena and Hermes, showed that heroes often succeed with the gods' favor. This dynamic underscores the Greek belief in synergy between mortal effort and divine grace.

10.9.2 Inevitable Destiny

From the moment of Perseus's conception, the prophecy about Acrisius's death loomed. Every attempt to circumvent fate led inexorably to its fulfillment. This motif recurs across Greek myths: resisting destiny can bring about the very outcome one dreads. Accepting fate with humility often proves the best path, emphasizing the tragic or instructive dimension of Greek storytelling.

10.9.3 Responsibility of Power

With Medusa's head, Perseus gained a terrifying weapon. While he used it to save Andromeda and punish evil kings, the power to turn living beings to stone was morally complex. Perseus's occasional reliance on the Gorgon's head for lethal solutions raises questions about **justice vs. mercy**—a reminder that even heroic power can be perilous if not wielded with restraint. Greek myths frequently explore the fine line between righteous retribution and excessive violence.

10.10 Cultural Influence of the Perseus Myth

10.10.1 Artistic Representations

In ancient Greek art, **Perseus** was a frequent subject. Vase paintings, temple friezes, and sculptures depicted his encounters with Medusa, the moment of beheading, or his rescue of Andromeda. These scenes captured the drama of man vs. monster, as well as the elegance of winged sandals or the chilling imagery of a snake-haired Gorgon. Temple dedications sometimes referenced Perseus's bravery as a model of piety—he overcame monstrous evils with the help of the gods.

10.10.2 Foundational Tales for Cities

Various Greek city-states claimed ties to Perseus's lineage, weaving his feats into local traditions. For example, Mycenae viewed him as a founder-figure or an important ancestor. These genealogies provided a blend of **myth and civic identity**, with the city's greatness tracing back to the hero's divine parentage and triumphs. Theater performances, religious festivals, and family rites often evoked Perseus's deeds, reinforcing communal pride and moral lessons.

10.11 Comparison with Other Heroes

Perseus's story stands alongside those of **Theseus**, **Heracles**, and others:

- **Theseus** overcame the Minotaur with cunning, but he mostly relied on mortal help (Ariadne's thread). Perseus, by contrast, directly received multiple **divine artifacts**, reflecting a higher level of direct godly intervention.
- **Heracles** performed labors to atone for wrongdoing, showcasing strength and endurance. Perseus's challenges centered more on **destiny** and **self-defense**—his mission to obtain Medusa's head was forced upon him, not a penance for personal guilt.
- **Odysseus** excelled in strategy across numerous trials, often facing moral dilemmas. Perseus's morality is less questioned—he acts out of necessity or justice, though the stony fate of his enemies can appear ruthless.

By seeing these distinctions, we appreciate the variety within Greek hero myths. No single pattern of heroism rules them all. Each hero's journey tests different virtues and vices, weaving a broad tapestry of what it means to strive under the watchful eyes of the gods.

CHAPTER 11

Theseus and the Minotaur

11.1 Introduction: A Hero for Athens

Among the pantheon of Greek heroes, **Theseus** stands out as the champion of Athens. While Perseus and Heracles undertook quests across far-flung lands, Theseus's most famous victory occurred closer to home—on the island of Crete—yet it profoundly shaped the destiny of Athens. His triumph over the **Minotaur**, a savage creature lurking in a labyrinth, signified not just personal bravery but also the rise of Athens as a respected power among Greek city-states.

This chapter examines how Theseus grew from a determined young prince into a symbol of Athenian strength. We will follow his early life, his volunteering to slay the Minotaur, and his journey through the **Labyrinth**, as well as the tragic events that concluded his voyage. Themes of **courage**, **cleverness**, and **responsibility** run through this narrative, teaching lessons about leadership, family ties, and the moral cost of triumph.

11.2 Background: King Minos and the Island of Crete

11.2.1 Minos's Rise to Power

Long before Theseus was born, Crete was ruled by **King Minos**, a son of Zeus (in the form of a bull) and Europa. According to myth, Minos gained his throne with the gods' help. He boasted that Poseidon favored him by sending a majestic white bull from the sea, a sign of Minos's right to rule. Supposedly, Minos was meant to sacrifice this bull back to Poseidon in gratitude. However, once he saw how splendid it was, he decided to keep it in his herds, offering a lesser bull to the god instead.

This **deception** enraged Poseidon. In response, the sea god cursed Minos's wife, **Pasiphaë**, causing her to develop a bizarre passion for the bull. From that unnatural union came the **Minotaur**, a beast with a bull's head and a man's body. Horrified yet unwilling to kill the creature, Minos sought to hide his family's shame while keeping the Minotaur contained.

11.2.2 Daedalus and the Labyrinth

Minos commanded **Daedalus**, a renowned inventor and architect, to construct a prison from which the Minotaur could never escape. Daedalus built the **Labyrinth**—a sprawling maze of twisting passages so complex that anyone entering risked wandering forever. Deep within this subterranean structure, the Minotaur roamed, feeding on flesh provided by Minos as tribute or from those unluckily cast into the Labyrinth's darkness.

Over time, tales of the Minotaur spread, making Crete both feared and respected. The labyrinth itself came to symbolize **entrapment** and human cunning. Minos, while maintaining power, had to manage the shame of the beast's existence, balancing fear and secrecy to ensure no internal rebellion. Such was the state of Crete when Athens became entangled in its affairs.

11.3 Athens Under Tribute: The Roots of a Grudge

11.3.1 Androgeus's Death

King Minos's conflict with Athens began with the death of his son, **Androgeus**. Some versions say that Androgeus traveled to Athens and excelled in the city's athletic games, provoking envy or political conspiracies that led to his murder. Another version suggests he was sent to fight a dangerous bull on behalf of the Athenians and perished. Regardless of the exact cause, Minos blamed Athens for his son's death. Outraged, he launched a war or demanded a crippling punishment to avenge Androgeus.

11.3.2 The Dreaded Tribute

In most retellings, Athens lost to Crete or sought to avoid a full-scale invasion by striking a humiliating deal. Every **nine years** (or sometimes yearly, depending on the source), Athens had to send a tribute of seven young men and seven young women to Crete. These youths were given to the **Minotaur**. The arrangement was not only a massive emotional blow to the Athenian people, who faced the sorrow of losing their children, but also a political statement of Crete's supremacy. For Athenians, it was a source of deep shame and smoldering resentment, setting the stage for a hero to rise and break this cruel cycle.

11.4 The Early Life of Theseus

11.4.1 Parentage and the Sword Under the Rock

Theseus was born under peculiar circumstances. His father, **Aegeus**, King of Athens, visited the wise king Pittheus in Troezen. After being advised that he could secure an heir, Aegeus spent a night with Pittheus's daughter, **Aethra**. Some versions claim Poseidon also had a role in Theseus's conception, but most emphasize Aegeus as the mortal father.

Before leaving, Aegeus placed his **sword and sandals** under a massive rock, instructing Aethra that if she bore a son who could lift the stone, he should claim those items and journey to Athens to find his father. Growing up, Theseus eventually performed that feat, proving his strength. He set off to Athens, traveling by land rather than sea because he wanted to face dangers and prove himself worthy of the throne.

11.4.2 Roadside Adventures and Tests

On his way to Athens, Theseus encountered a series of bandits and monsters terrorizing travelers. Notable figures included **Periphetes**, the Club-Bearer, whom Theseus defeated, taking his weapon. Another was **Sciron**, a robber who made travelers wash his feet before kicking them into the sea to be devoured by a giant turtle. Each time, Theseus overcame these villains, often turning their own methods against them—reflecting a principle of **just retribution**.

By the time Theseus arrived in Athens, he was famed for clearing the coastal road of threats, making travel safer. This display of heroism built his reputation as a champion of the people. Yet, upon meeting King Aegeus, Theseus faced the suspicion of Aegeus's new wife, Medea, who feared for her own children's inheritance. Ultimately, Aegeus recognized the sword and sandals, accepting Theseus as his son and heir, but new dangers awaited when it came time for Athens to deliver its tribute to Crete.

11.5 The Decision to Face the Minotaur

11.5.1 The Third Tribute

The cycle of tributes to Crete continued, marking times of profound grief in Athens. When the third round of hostages was due, Theseus could not bear the idea of seeing more innocent youths sacrificed. He volunteered to join them, swearing to slay the Minotaur and end the tributes for good. Some stories say the Athenians tried to dissuade him, but Theseus insisted. King Aegeus agreed with sorrow, reminding his son to return with **white sails** if he succeeded. If he failed, the black sails under which he left would signal his death.

This pact set the stage for one of the greatest feats in Greek myth. Theseus, an **outsider** to Crete, would challenge the monstrous offspring of Pasiphaë and the bull—an impossible threat at the heart of a labyrinth built to contain it. In this mission, Theseus embodied Athenian **defiance** against oppression, turning a forced tribute into a chance for liberation.

11.5.2 The Departure

The chosen seven young men and seven young women boarded a black-sailed ship with Theseus at their head. Accounts differ on how the tributes reacted: some were resigned to their fate, others placed desperate hope in Theseus's bravery. Aegeus watched from the shore, grieving yet proud. He pinned his hopes on the promise of victory. The entire city prayed for Theseus, seeing him as the best chance to end the savage arrangement with Crete.

11.6 Arrival on Crete: Under King Minos's Eye

11.6.1 A Tense Welcome

When Theseus and the tributes arrived at Knossos—the grand palace of Minos—Cretan guards herded them with cold efficiency. King Minos was proud, certain that the Labyrinth made any attempt at rebellion pointless. The Athenians would provide fresh meat for the Minotaur, upholding the terms of tribute. A single misstep could provoke the Cretan soldiers to kill Theseus on the spot.

Yet beneath Minos's arrogance lurked an unspoken shame about his monstrous stepson, hidden from the world's eyes. Despite this, or perhaps because of it, Minos liked to display his dominance over Athens. Publicly sacrificing these youths to the beast served as a stark message to all who questioned Crete's power.

11.6.2 Daedalus's Secret Knowledge

Observing from within the palace was **Daedalus**, the genius who built the Labyrinth. He understood its winding corridors better than anyone. Some versions suggest Daedalus felt guilt or pity for the victims thrown to the Minotaur. Others say he was secretly resentful of Minos's oppressive control. Though he did not openly defy the king, Daedalus's knowledge would prove crucial to Theseus's success—though indirectly, through another Cretan who took pity on the Athenian hero.

11.7 Ariadne: Minos's Daughter and Theseus's Ally

11.7.1 Love at First Sight

Ariadne, daughter of Minos and Pasiphaë, beheld Theseus among the tributes. Smitten by his courage and appearance, she resolved to help him. She could not stand idly by, watching him and his companions perish. Some say Aphrodite inspired her love; others claim Ariadne was moved by Theseus's sheer audacity. Regardless, she approached him in secret, promising aid if he would pledge to take her away from Crete.

11.7.2 The Ball of Thread

Ariadne turned to Daedalus or used her own ingenuity to offer Theseus a **simple but vital tool**: a ball of thread, sometimes called **"Ariadne's Thread."** The plan was straightforward: Theseus would tie one end of the thread at the Labyrinth's entrance and unravel it as he went deeper, ensuring he could retrace his steps. This solution turned the infinite confusion of the maze into a single winding path—assuming Theseus survived his encounter with the Minotaur.

This moment is among the most famous in Greek myth, symbolizing how resourcefulness can conquer even the most cunning traps. The labyrinth that seemed impossible to navigate was undone by a simple spool of thread and the trust between Theseus and Ariadne.

11.8 Entering the Labyrinth

11.8.1 Stepping into Darkness

That night or the following day, depending on the version, guards led Theseus and the tributes to the Labyrinth's gates. Traditionally, the others stayed near the entrance while Theseus ventured alone to find the Minotaur. By tying Ariadne's thread at the entrance, he slowly advanced deeper, letting the thin line unspool behind him. The walls were high and the air stagnant, with countless dead-ends branching away. In the dim torchlight, every footstep echoed ominously.

The labyrinth tested more than physical prowess. One wrong turn, a moment of panic, and Theseus would be lost forever. Yet he pressed on, mind fixed on both the Minotaur's destruction and the possibility of deliverance for all Athenians.

11.8.2 Facing Fear

As he advanced, bones scattered the floor—remnants of past victims. A dreadful stench hung in the corridors, reminding Theseus of the creature's carnivorous nature. Greek storytellers emphasized the **psychological** challenge: Theseus had to remain calm, keep track of the thread, and ready his sword. The beast could lurk around any corner. Yet the hero's confidence did not waver. He recalled his father's sorrow and Ariadne's trust, fueling his determination.

11.9 Battle with the Minotaur

11.9.1 The Monstrous Form

Eventually, Theseus found himself in a vast chamber where he heard the Minotaur's heavy breathing. The creature loomed in the half-light—a towering form with a bull's head and powerful human body. Some myths describe the Minotaur as savage yet oddly sorrowful, a product of unnatural birth, forever imprisoned by Minos's pride. Others portray it as pure brute force, possessed only by hunger and rage.

11.9.2 A Fight of Wits and Strength

The Minotaur charged, horns lowered. Theseus dodged to the side, using the labyrinth's pillars for cover. The beast's strength was immense. One direct blow could finish the hero. Yet Theseus's skill and cunning in close combat, honed from previous exploits against bandits, gave him an edge. He danced around the monster, avoiding its horns and driving quick strikes with his sword.

In some accounts, the Minotaur momentarily pinned Theseus against a wall, nearly crushing him. Through agility and swift reflexes, Theseus stabbed the beast in a vital spot. The Minotaur roared, lashing out in its death throes. Finally, with a well-placed thrust, Theseus **slew the monster**, ending the threat. Exhausted and relieved, he knelt beside the beast's colossal form, blood staining the labyrinth floor.

11.9.3 Escape from the Labyrinth

Victorious but pressed for time, Theseus followed the thread back. The labyrinth was still a maze of twisting halls, but the line of thread guided him unerringly. Reaching the entrance, he rejoined the terrified Athenian youths. Together, they fled the labyrinth, sealing it behind them. Outside, Ariadne waited, eager to escape Crete alongside Theseus. The day was far from over, though, for King Minos would soon discover his monstrous guardian was dead.

11.10 Flight from Crete: Triumph and Tragedy

11.10.1 A Narrow Escape

When Minos learned of the Minotaur's demise, his fury was boundless. Betrayal by his own daughter stung him deeply. Some stories suggest Minos tried to pursue the fleeing Athenians, but Theseus acted swiftly. He and the rescued youths seized a ship, bringing Ariadne on board. The black sails remained hoisted, as they had no time to switch them. Under cover of darkness or with a favorable wind from the gods, they left Crete behind.

As the ship cut across the waves, Theseus likely felt a surge of pride. He had ended the tributes, liberated the threatened youths, and proven Athens could not be subjugated by Crete's monstrous secrets. Yet fate had a twist awaiting him—his dealings with Ariadne and the watchful gods would yield consequences.

11.10.2 The Abandonment of Ariadne

A famous twist in the myth concerns how Ariadne was **left behind** on the island of Naxos. Accounts vary:

- Some say Athena or another god commanded Theseus to abandon Ariadne, claiming she was destined to marry the god Dionysus.
- Others suggest Theseus acted out of forgetfulness or a change of heart.
- A few sources imply Ariadne herself fell asleep, and Theseus departed unknowingly.

Whatever the reason, Ariadne awoke to find Theseus gone, stricken with grief. Meanwhile, Dionysus (in many stories) arrived, comforting Ariadne and eventually making her his wife. This bittersweet outcome reveals Theseus's flawed side. Though a hero, he is not immune to decisions that hurt others—reflecting a broader lesson that even great victories can be stained by personal failings.

11.11 The Black Sails: King Aegeus's Final Grief

11.11.1 Return to Athens

Buoyed by success yet bearing a heavy heart about Ariadne, Theseus continued home. He and the surviving youths approached Athens, expecting a joyful reunion with King Aegeus. However, Theseus overlooked or neglected his father's instruction about changing the sails from black to white if he returned in triumph. Some say he was too lost in thought about Ariadne's abandonment; others argue a sense of triumph or exhaustion distracted him.

11.11.2 The Tragic Leap

King Aegeus, gazing from a cliff to watch for his son's ship, spotted the **black sails**. Consumed by despair, he assumed Theseus had died. In heartbreak, Aegeus **threw himself into the sea**, which thereafter was called the **Aegean Sea**. Upon landing, Theseus learned of his father's death. Though he saved Athens from the Minotaur, his forgetfulness caused a personal tragedy. This sorrow underscored a central Greek principle: even a hero's greatest success can be marred by small oversights or fate's cruelty.

11.12 The Reign of Theseus and His Legacy

11.12.1 King of Athens

With Aegeus gone, Theseus became King of Athens. He strove to unify Attica, championing reforms that promoted greater equality among citizens. In some stories, he reorganized Athens's political structure, seeking to ensure fairness and stability. While the historical accuracy of these reforms is debated, myths credit Theseus with turning Athens into a model city-state, guided by reason, justice, and communal values.

11.12.2 A Complex Hero

Throughout his rule, Theseus engaged in further adventures—helping the Argives bury their dead after the war of the Seven Against Thebes, or journeying to the Amazons. Yet his character remained **multi-layered**. He was a champion of the oppressed but sometimes rash, as with Ariadne's abandonment. He sought to do good for his people, but personal flaws led to rifts in his own life. Finally, Theseus's death came under ambiguous circumstances—some say he was cast from a cliff by a rival king, marking a lonely end for the hero who once bested the Minotaur.

11.12.3 Lessons from the Labyrinth

The slaying of the Minotaur taught future generations that cunning and moral conviction can conquer monstrous evils. Yet it also revealed how the journey of a hero is rarely without **sacrifice and sorrow**—Ariadne's abandonment and Aegeus's death both occurred as direct results of Theseus's quest. Within Greek culture, Theseus symbolized a **proud Athenian identity**, championing freedom from tyranny. At the same time, his story served as a warning about forgetting promises and underestimating the power of fate.

CHAPTER 12

Hercules and His Twelve Labors

12.1 Introduction: The Strongest of Heroes

Hercules (in Greek, **Heracles**) is perhaps the most renowned figure in Greek mythology, famed for his **superhuman strength** and enduring spirit. Born from Zeus and a mortal woman, Hercules walked a path marked by divine opposition—particularly from Zeus's wife, **Hera**—and by his own moral challenges. His story reveals how even extraordinary power does not shield one from suffering, guilt, or the need for redemption.

The centerpiece of Hercules's myth is the **Twelve Labors**, a series of seemingly impossible tasks imposed upon him as **atonement** for a tragic crime. Across these labors, Hercules battled savage creatures, journeyed to distant lands, and outwitted forces beyond mortal comprehension. This chapter details each labor and the lessons they impart, showing how Greek myths wove heroism, remorse, and the quest for purification into a single, grand narrative.

12.2 Origins: A Child of Zeus and the Wrath of Hera

12.2.1 The Birth of Hercules

Hercules's mother, **Alcmene**, was a mortal princess married to Amphitryon. Zeus, enthralled by Alcmene's beauty, disguised himself as her husband one night, resulting in Hercules's conception. Hera, Zeus's wife, seethed with jealousy upon discovering this affair. She harbored a lifelong grudge against Hercules, seeking to thwart him at every turn.

At birth, Hera tried to delay Hercules's arrival so that another child, **Eurystheus**, born of a royal line, would precede Hercules and claim a prophecy granting dominion. This cunning trick worked—Eurystheus entered the world first, becoming King of Mycenae. Hercules, though eventually recognized for his strength, was destined to serve Eurystheus, fulfilling a bitter cosmic arrangement shaped by Hera's malice and Zeus's infidelity.

12.2.2 Early Trials: The Serpents in the Cradle

Even as an infant, Hercules faced Hera's wrath. Legend says Hera sent two serpents into his cradle, hoping they would kill him. Instead, baby Hercules displayed his **divine strength** by strangling the serpents with his tiny hands. This event foreshadowed the hero's future, indicating that while Hera's hostility would never cease, Hercules's might would enable him to survive and perform feats unimaginable to ordinary mortals.

12.3 A Tragic Crime and the Need for Atonement

12.3.1 Madness from Hera

Hercules grew into a formidable warrior, marrying **Megara**, a Theban princess. They had children and found happiness. But Hera devised another plan to torment him: she struck Hercules with a fit of **madness**, causing him to confuse his family for enemies. In a frenzy, Hercules killed his wife and children, an act that would scar him forever once he regained his senses.

This ghastly deed, though not his fault, demanded atonement by Greek moral standards. The hero, devastated, approached the Oracle of Delphi for guidance. The Oracle instructed him to serve King Eurystheus—Hera's chosen instrument—and perform whatever labors he commanded. Only through these tasks could Hercules cleanse his conscience and regain peace.

12.3.2 Obedience to Eurystheus

Now bound by the gods' decree, Hercules reported to Eurystheus in Mycenae. Eurystheus, a timid king overshadowed by Hercules's reputation, relished this chance to control his mighty cousin. Hoping to see Hercules fail—or die—he assigned challenges that seemed impossible. Hera quietly supported Eurystheus's demands, ensuring they grew more perilous each time. Thus began the **Twelve Labors**, each a step on a journey that tested not only Hercules's strength but also his capacity for endurance, cunning, and humility.

12.4 The Nemean Lion (First Labor)

12.4.1 The Invulnerable Hide

Eurystheus first sent Hercules to slay the **Nemean Lion**, a beast terrorizing the region of Nemea. This lion's **golden fur** was said to be impenetrable by normal weapons. Arrows bounced off it. Spears broke against its hide. Hercules soon discovered that direct combat with normal tools was futile. The lion retreated into a cave with two entrances, escaping any attempt at a clean kill.

12.4.2 Wrestling the Beast

In a cunning move, Hercules blocked one entrance, forcing the lion into a single exit. There, he cornered the beast, discarding his useless weapons and **strangling** it with his bare hands. Upon victory, he tried to skin the lion using normal blades, but none worked. Eventually, Hercules used the lion's own **claws** to slice its pelt, fashioning a cloak that granted him near-invincibility.

Carrying the lion's carcass as proof, Hercules returned to Eurystheus. The king, frightened by this display, forbade Hercules from entering the city gates with his trophies. From then on, he commanded Hercules to show his successes outside the walls. The Nemean Lion's pelt became the hero's iconic outfit, symbolizing how **brute force**, tempered with problem-solving, could conquer even invulnerable foes.

12.5 The Lernaean Hydra (Second Labor)

12.5.1 The Many-Headed Monster

Next, Eurystheus sent Hercules to kill the **Hydra** near Lake Lerna. The Hydra was a serpentine monster with multiple heads—often said to be nine, though some versions say more. Its central head was immortal, and any severed head would **regrow two more** if cut off without special measures. As if that was not enough, the Hydra's very breath was poisonous.

12.5.2 Fire and Cunning

Hercules did not face the Hydra alone. He enlisted his nephew, **Iolaus**, to help. After luring the creature from its den, Hercules sliced off heads one by one, while Iolaus quickly **cauterized** each neck stump with a torch, preventing regeneration. Eventually, only the immortal head remained, which Hercules pinned under a massive rock, ending its threat.

However, Eurystheus, seeing Iolaus's involvement, argued that the labor should not fully count since Hercules did not act alone. Moreover, Hercules harvested the Hydra's **toxic blood** to dip his arrows in, a choice that would prove pivotal—and sometimes tragic—in future adventures. This labor underscored the role of **teamwork** and cunning in Greek myths, while also hinting that victory can lead to moral dilemmas when lethal powers are claimed.

12.6 The Ceryneian Hind (Third Labor)

12.6.1 Sacred to Artemis

Eurystheus's third command was to capture, alive, the **Ceryneian Hind**—a swift, golden-horned deer sacred to the goddess Artemis.

The task was to prove more than just strength. If Hercules harmed the hind, he risked angering the goddess of the hunt. Eurystheus hoped the hero would fail or provoke divine wrath.

12.6.2 A Year-Long Chase

Hercules spent **one full year** pursuing the hind, never risking a direct wound. He tracked it across mountains and forests, waiting for the right moment to snare it gently. Eventually, he caught the deer near a river. Artemis appeared, indignant that her sacred animal was taken. Hercules pleaded that he meant no harm and only acted under forced servitude. Moved by his explanation (and, in some versions, by Zeus's subtle influence), Artemis allowed him to show the hind to Eurystheus, then release it unharmed.

This episode illustrated Hercules's **patience** and **respect for the gods**, crucial elements in a world where brute strength alone might backfire if it offended a deity.

12.7 The Erymanthian Boar (Fourth Labor)

12.7.1 A Mountain Terror

The next task was to capture the **Erymanthian Boar**, which ravaged farmland around Mount Erymanthus. This giant, wild boar was fearsome, capable of tearing apart hunters or flipping chariots with its tusks. Eurystheus demanded the creature be brought back alive, hoping the boar might kill Hercules or at least humiliate him.

12.7.2 Driving It into the Snow

Hercules used strategy: he chased the boar, exhausting it and herding it toward deep snowdrifts. Trapped by the heavy drifts, the boar slowed, allowing Hercules to snare it with chains. Proud of his success, he carried the roaring boar to Mycenae. Eurystheus, panicking at the sight, hid in a giant jar, refusing to come out. The comedic nature of the king's fear contrasted with Hercules's triumph, reflecting how **cowardice and arrogance** often coexist in the unworthy powerful.

12.8 The Augean Stables (Fifth Labor)

12.8.1 An Impossible Cleaning

In a departure from slaying monsters, Eurystheus ordered Hercules to **clean the Augean Stables** in a single day. These stables belonged to King Augeas of Elis, who owned vast herds. The stables had never been cleaned, piling up decades of filth. Eurystheus hoped to demean Hercules through menial labor that was physically impossible—moving mountains of manure in mere hours.

12.8.2 Rerouting Rivers

Hercules employed his trademark ingenuity: he **rerouted two nearby rivers**, the Alpheus and Peneus, so they rushed through the stables, washing away the filth in one massive surge. Augeas, furious that Hercules had completed the task by clever means, refused to honor a promised reward. Depending on the version, Hercules either marched back to Mycenae or later took vengeance on Augeas by waging war.

In either case, Eurystheus declared the labor invalid, claiming Hercules performed it for personal gain. The moral? Even heroic wits can be met with pettiness and broken promises. This event reinforced how cunning was just as threatening to the insecure Eurystheus as raw might.

12.9 The Stymphalian Birds (Sixth Labor)

12.9.1 Deadly Flocks

For the sixth labor, Hercules had to drive away or destroy the **Stymphalian Birds**. These man-eating creatures with metallic feathers plagued the region around Lake Stymphalia. They devoured crops and occasionally attacked villagers. But they nested in a marsh, difficult to approach without sinking in mud.

12.9.2 Rattling Bronze Clappers

Athena came to Hercules's aid, giving him **bronze clappers** (or a special rattle) forged by Hephaestus. Standing near the lake's edge, Hercules clashed these clappers together, creating a deafening noise that startled the birds into flight. As they rose, Hercules shot them down with arrows dipped in Hydra's venom or simply chased them away. Either outcome freed the region from a dangerous pest. This labor highlighted the power of **innovation**: sometimes, a little noise or a crafted tool can solve what brute force alone cannot.

12.10 The Cretan Bull (Seventh Labor)

12.10.1 Minos's Beast

Interestingly, this **Cretan Bull** might be the same bull Poseidon sent to King Minos—the very bull that fathered the Minotaur. Now it roamed Crete, laying waste to fields. Eurystheus ordered Hercules to capture it. Upon arriving on Crete, Hercules sought Minos's permission. Perhaps remembering the Minotaur fiasco, Minos refused to assist, though he did not impede Hercules's task.

12.10.2 Wrestling the Bull

Hercules cornered the bull, wrestled it to submission, then shipped it across the sea to Mycenae. Eurystheus, terrified once more, released the bull. It wandered near Marathon in Attica, becoming the infamous **Marathonian Bull**. This scattering of monstrous creatures was a recurring theme: while Hercules completed his tasks, sometimes the beasts ended up in new locales, causing different problems for others.

12.11 The Mares of Diomedes (Eighth Labor)

12.11.1 Flesh-Eating Horses

Next, Eurystheus commanded Hercules to retrieve the **Mares of Diomedes**, man-eating horses belonging to Diomedes, a Thracian king. These savage beasts feasted on captives and could not be tamed. Again, the labor tested Hercules's cunning and sense of justice, as Diomedes himself was cruel and tyrannical.

12.11.2 Feeding Diomedes to His Own Mares

In some versions, Hercules overpowered Diomedes's stable grooms, then turned on Diomedes himself. After subduing him in battle, Hercules threw Diomedes to the mares, which devoured their own master. The shock of this meal pacified the mares—no longer rampaging. Hercules then led them away. Eurystheus, upon seeing them, dedicated the horses to Hera or released them. The brutality of this labor revealed the **harsh justice** in Greek myth: Diomedes, a cruel owner, met a fate matching his vile practices.

12.12 The Belt (Girdle) of Hippolyta (Ninth Labor)

12.12.1 The Amazon Queen

For the ninth labor, Eurystheus demanded the **belt** (or girdle) of **Hippolyta**, queen of the Amazons—a formidable tribe of warrior women. The belt signified Hippolyta's royal authority. It was said that Eurystheus's daughter desired this trophy, prompting the king to send Hercules on a politically fraught mission.

12.12.2 Misunderstandings and Battle

Hippolyta initially welcomed Hercules, willing to give him the belt. However, Hera disguised herself among the Amazons, spreading rumors that Hercules planned to abduct the queen. The enraged Amazons attacked. In the ensuing battle, Hippolyta was killed (in some accounts) or forced to yield. Hercules seized the belt and escaped.

This labor presents a tragic dimension: an alliance might have formed, but **deception and mistrust** led to conflict. Greek myths often show how misunderstandings—especially when manipulated by jealous gods—doom potentially peaceful outcomes.

12.13 The Cattle of Geryon (Tenth Labor)

12.13.1 A Three-Headed Giant

The tenth labor took Hercules to the far west, near the edges of the known world, to seize the **cattle of Geryon**. Geryon was a fearsome giant with **three heads** (and in some tales, three bodies joined at the waist). He kept a herd of crimson-colored cattle guarded by a two-headed dog, **Orthrus**, and a herdsman named Eurytion.

12.13.2 Journey Across the World

To reach Geryon's land (often identified with Erytheia or a region near the Atlantic), Hercules crossed the deserts of Libya. The sun's heat tormented him, so he shot an arrow at Helios, the sun god, who admired such boldness and lent Hercules a golden cup to sail across the sea. Upon arriving, Hercules slew Orthrus, Eurytion, and finally Geryon in a massive confrontation. He herded the prized cattle back through Europe, facing more perils, including rebellious local kings.

Returning them to Eurystheus completed another formidable quest. This journey symbolized **exploration** and the bridging of distant lands, reflecting Greek curiosity about the edges of their known world.

12.14 The Apples of the Hesperides (Eleventh Labor)

12.14.1 Golden Apples and a Serpent

Eurystheus then tasked Hercules with acquiring **golden apples** from the Garden of the Hesperides. These apples were sacred to Hera, grown from a tree Earth (Gaia) gave her as a wedding gift. The orchard, guarded by the **Hesperides** (nymphs of the evening) and a fearsome serpent named **Ladon**, lay in a hidden location far to the west.

12.14.2 Enlisting Atlas

After a lengthy search, Hercules learned the Titan **Atlas**—who held up the sky—could fetch the apples, as he was the father of the Hesperides. Hercules offered to bear the sky if Atlas would pluck the apples. Atlas agreed, enjoying freedom from his cosmic burden. Once he returned with the apples, Atlas tried to leave Hercules holding the sky forever. Yet Hercules feigned an adjustment request, tricking Atlas into taking the sky back. He then seized the apples and left.

This cunning exchange showcased Hercules's **intellect**. Despite being famed for muscle, he outwitted a Titan. But upon returning, Eurystheus could not keep the apples since they belonged to the gods. Athena took them back, emphasizing that while mortals might accomplish wonders, they cannot hold divine gifts indefinitely.

12.15 The Capture of Cerberus (Twelfth Labor)

12.15.1 Descent into the Underworld

The final labor was the most daunting: **capture Cerberus**, the three-headed guard dog of the Underworld, without using weapons. This forced Hercules to venture into Hades's domain, a place where no mortal could walk freely without risk of eternal imprisonment.

12.15.2 Overpowering the Guard Dog

Aided by Hermes or Athena, Hercules entered the Underworld. He encountered the spirits of the dead, including heroes like Theseus or possibly his own relatives. Eventually, he found **Hades**, requesting permission to take Cerberus. Hades consented—on condition that Hercules subdue the beast with no weapons. Hercules wrestled Cerberus, grappling its snapping jaws and serpentine tail until the hound submitted.

Bringing Cerberus to Eurystheus, Hercules completed the Twelfth Labor. After proving the dog's capture, he returned Cerberus to the Underworld. With this final triumph, the gods and oracles deemed Hercules's **atonement** fulfilled. He had conquered beasts, defied gods, and redeemed his terrible crime. The cycle of labors ended, granting him inner peace—at least for a time.

12.16 After the Labors: Achievements and Sorrows

12.16.1 Further Adventures

Though the Twelve Labors were done, Hercules's life continued to brim with feats. He joined expeditions like the **Argonauts** in some versions, fought giants, and defended kingdoms. His legend grew to overshadow nearly all other heroes of Greece. Yet personal misfortunes still haunted him. Another marriage led to tragedy when his wife Deianeira, tricked into using the **tainted blood** of the centaur Nessus as a love charm, caused Hercules excruciating torment.

12.16.2 Death and Apotheosis

Dying from the poisoned garment, Hercules built a funeral pyre. As flames consumed his mortal body, the gods lifted his spirit to **Mount Olympus**, granting him immortality. Even Hera reconciled with him, giving him her daughter Hebe as a bride in the divine realm. Thus, Hercules achieved what few mortals could: **apotheosis**, or elevation to godhood. This end symbolized the ultimate reward for a hero who had suffered, atoned, and proven his worth through countless hardships.

12.17 Themes and Lessons from Hercules

12.17.1 Atonement and Redemption

Hercules's story is unique among Greek heroes for its direct link to **atonement**. Rather than slaying monsters for glory alone, he performed the labors under command, driven by guilt for his own tragic actions. This framework painted heroism as more than conquest; it was **moral restitution**. No matter how mighty a hero, personal demons demanded resolution through effort, humility, and perseverance.

12.17.2 Strength and Intellect Combined

While Hercules's primary attribute is physical strength, several labors highlight the necessity of **strategy**—rerouting rivers, using fire to stop the Hydra's regrowth, or tricking Atlas. Greek culture admired cunning, but Hercules's brand of cleverness was often direct and rooted in practical sense, different from the refined guile of, say, Odysseus.

12.17.3 Divine Influence, Human Will

Hercules's struggles with Hera underscore the role gods played in shaping mortal destinies. At the same time, the hero's **determination** allowed him to transcend curses and punishments. Greek mythology often emphasizes that while gods can impose trials, a hero's response—courage or despair—belongs to the mortal alone. Hercules stands as an emblem of enduring one's burdens and emerging stronger, though not unscathed.

12.18 Cultural Impact of Hercules

12.18.1 Hero Cults and Worship

Across Greece, Hercules was **venerated** in temples and shrines, receiving honors closer to those of a minor god. People prayed to him for protection or invoked his name when facing great physical challenges. This worship sometimes included athletic competitions, echoing the heroic feats that tested one's body and spirit.

12.18.2 A Model of Virtue and Warning

Hercules's name became synonymous with **strength**. His lion-skin cloak and club remain iconic symbols in art, sculpted on temple metopes and painted on pottery. Yet his story also served as a **moral reminder** that unrestrained power or uncontrollable rage could destroy even beloved figures. Children studying Homeric or post-Homeric literature learned from Hercules's accomplishments—and from his torments—that heroism does not exempt one from tragedy or moral responsibility.

12.19 Conclusion of Chapter 12

Hercules's Twelve Labors encapsulate the **breadth of Greek heroism**—monsters, tasks of cunning, journeys to remote edges of the world, and the confrontation of supernatural powers. More importantly, they represent a soul's struggle to **amend a terrible guilt** through service and endurance. Each labor tested not only Hercules's body but also his will to persist despite personal anguish, divine hostility, and lethal opposition.

The outcome—apotheosis—demonstrates a unique resolution: a mortal rising to join the gods. Hercules's narrative thus offers hope that even grievous sins can be set right through steadfast effort. In Greek society, these labors taught moral perseverance, the interplay of cunning and strength, and the acceptance of a destiny shaped by both mortal choice and divine plans.

CHAPTER 13

Jason and the Argonauts

13.1 Introduction: The Quest for the Golden Fleece

Among the epic quests in Greek mythology, few are as famous as **Jason and the Argonauts** in their search for the **Golden Fleece**. This adventure involves a band of heroes sailing on the ship **Argo** to distant lands, facing monsters, storms, and betrayal. At its heart, the story is about **bravery** and **teamwork**, as well as the unpredictable role of the gods in mortal affairs.

Jason's quest to reclaim his rightful throne by retrieving the Golden Fleece is both thrilling and tragic. His success depends on forming alliances—both with fellow heroes and with Medea, a powerful sorceress who becomes his partner and, later, a figure of heartbreak. This chapter explores the background of Jason's royal family, the legendary crew of the Argo, the trials they encounter, and the tragic cost of victory. While the main focus is on daring feats and cunning solutions, the tale ultimately reminds us that ambition can lead to betrayal and sorrow if not handled with care.

13.2 The Golden Fleece and Its Origins

13.2.1 Phrixus and the Flying Ram

The **Golden Fleece** traces back to a boy named **Phrixus** and his sister **Helle**, children of King Athamas. Their stepmother threatened their lives, so the gods sent a **golden-fleeced ram** to rescue them. The ram carried Phrixus and Helle through the sky. Sadly, Helle fell into the sea (later called the Hellespont) and drowned, but Phrixus arrived safely in **Colchis**, a distant kingdom on the eastern shore of the Black Sea.

Grateful to King Aeëtes of Colchis for shelter, Phrixus sacrificed the ram to the gods and gave its shimmering fleece to Aeëtes. Aeëtes hung the **Golden Fleece** in a sacred grove, guarded by a sleepless dragon. Over time, the fleece came to symbolize **authority** and **divine favor**. Many believed whoever possessed it would gain prosperity or a rightful claim to power, which explains why Jason's quest for the fleece is key to regaining his stolen throne.

13.2.2 The Fleece as a Symbol

While the fleece was literally a trophy in Colchis, it also stood for the **blessing of the gods**. By commanding Jason to bring it home, his uncle set a seemingly impossible demand that tested whether Jason was truly favored by the divine. This detail connects the quest to a recurring Greek idea: to accomplish great deeds, a hero must have both **courage** and **some measure of divine support**.

13.3 Jason's Early Life: The Stolen Throne

13.3.1 Pelias and the Prophecy

Jason was born the son of **Aeson**, rightful king of **Iolcus**. However, Aeson's half-brother, **Pelias**, usurped the throne. An oracle warned Pelias to beware a man wearing only one sandal—a sign that he would overthrow Pelias. Thus, Pelias lived in fear, suspecting every stranger who arrived in Iolcus.

13.3.2 Jason's Return and the Lost Sandal

Meanwhile, Jason grew up hidden from Pelias's reach. When he came of age, he journeyed to reclaim his birthright. On the way to Iolcus, he helped an old woman (actually the goddess Hera in disguise) cross a river, losing one sandal in the process. Arriving at the court with only one sandal, he immediately caught Pelias's attention. Pelias then challenged him: if Jason could bring back the Golden Fleece from Colchis—a feat no one believed possible—Pelias might yield the throne. Jason accepted, motivated by **honor** and **a rightful claim**.

13.4 Gathering the Argonauts

13.4.1 Building the Argo

To undertake the dangerous voyage, Jason needed a sturdy ship and loyal companions. He commissioned **Argus**, a skilled shipwright, to build a special vessel named the **Argo** (derived from Argus's name). Athena herself blessed the Argo, placing a **talking beam** from the sacred oak of Dodona in its prow. This magical plank could sometimes give warnings or advice, hinting that the gods supported Jason's quest.

13.4.2 Famous Crew Members

Jason assembled a remarkable crew, later called the **Argonauts**, or "sailors of the Argo." The roster varies by source, but it often includes:

- **Heracles (Hercules)**: The mightiest Greek hero, though some versions say he left the journey early.
- **Orpheus**: A gifted musician whose songs could charm beasts and even stones.
- **Castor and Polydeuces (Pollux)**: Twin brothers known as the Dioscuri, famed for their boxing and horse-taming skills.
- **Atalanta** (in some versions): A swift huntress, though certain tales exclude her.
- **Argus**: The ship's builder, skilled at repairs and navigation.
- **Meleager**: A valiant warrior known for the Calydonian Boar Hunt.
- **Lynceus**: Said to have extraordinary eyesight, able to see through obstacles.

This diverse group blended **strength**, **cunning**, **music**, and **craftsmanship**, reflecting the importance of multiple talents in Greek heroic ventures. Each Argonaut contributed unique gifts vital for overcoming the trials ahead.

13.5 Setting Sail: Early Adventures

13.5.1 The Isle of Lemnos

Their first major stop was **Lemnos**, an island inhabited only by women after a tragic event where they had driven away or slain their menfolk. Initially wary of the arriving heroes, the Lemnian women soon welcomed the Argonauts. A short period of intermingling followed, with some Argonauts fathering children there. But Heracles, who remained focused on the quest, scolded them for delays. Eventually, they departed, continuing their journey eastward.

13.5.2 The Doliones and Cyzicus

Further along, they landed among the **Doliones**, ruled by King Cyzicus. The Argonauts received hospitality, but soon, unknown to either side, they were separated by storms and darkness. In a terrible twist, the Doliones mistook the returning Argonauts for enemies at night, and a battle erupted. King Cyzicus died in the confusion. Heartbroken upon learning of the mistake, the Argonauts performed funeral rites. This tragedy underscores the **fragility of alliances** when communication falters, a theme often repeated in Greek tales.

13.6 Phineus and the Harpies: A Test of Compassion

13.6.1 The Blind Prophet's Torment

Eventually, the Argonauts reached **Salmydessus**, home of the blind prophet **Phineus**. Phineus was cursed by the gods—each time he tried to eat, monstrous **Harpies** swooped in, snatching his food or fouling it, leaving him starving. Despite his suffering, Phineus retained his gift of prophecy, able to see the future more clearly than any mortal.

13.6.2 The Sons of the North Wind

Two Argonauts, **Zetes and Calais**, were sons of Boreas (the North Wind), gifted with the ability to fly. They chased the Harpies away from Phineus, freeing him from torment. In gratitude, Phineus revealed crucial advice: the route to Colchis was blocked by the **Clashing Rocks** (Symplegades), huge rocks that crashed together, pulverizing anything passing between them. Phineus instructed the Argonauts on how to safely navigate this lethal strait. This kindness rewarded compassion: by helping Phineus, they gained vital knowledge to survive.

13.7 The Clashing Rocks

13.7.1 Testing with a Dove

Following Phineus's guidance, the Argonauts approached the **Clashing Rocks**. As soon as anything tried to pass, the rocks would slam shut. Phineus advised Jason to release a **dove** first. If the bird passed through with only minor injury to its tail feathers, the Argonauts could immediately row behind it and slip through the moment the rocks recoiled.

13.7.2 A Narrow Escape

The plan worked. The dove lost some feathers, but made it through. The Argonauts rowed with all their might, and with the help of **Athena**, the Argo rushed forward. Though the rocks nearly crushed the ship's stern, the Argo emerged with minimal damage. After that, the Symplegades were said to stand still forever, no longer posing a danger. This dramatic passage illustrated how **strategy** and **divine favor** were often the difference between life and death.

13.8 Arrival in Colchis: Facing King Aeëtes

13.8.1 Tension at the Court

Having survived countless ordeals, the Argonauts finally reached **Colchis,** where the Golden Fleece hung. King **Aeëtes,** son of the sun god Helios, welcomed them cautiously. When Jason respectfully requested the fleece, Aeëtes grew suspicious, suspecting they intended to steal it. Aeëtes demanded Jason perform a series of **impossible tasks** if he wanted the fleece, hoping to see him fail.

13.8.2 The Tasks Set by Aeëtes

Aeëtes listed the following challenges:

1. **Yoke Fire-Breathing Bulls**: Two colossal bulls with bronze hooves and flaming breath had to be harnessed to a plow.

2. **Plow a Field and Sow Dragon's Teeth**: After plowing, Jason must plant the dragon's teeth. From these seeds would sprout armed warriors.
3. **Defeat the Earthborn Warriors**: The newly sprouted fighters would attack Jason at once.

If Jason survived all this, Aeëtes might allow him to take the fleece. Aeëtes did not expect success, certain that these tasks would overwhelm any mortal. But an unexpected ally emerged from Aeëtes's own family—his daughter, **Medea**.

13.9 Medea: Sorceress and Princess

13.9.1 Love and Loyalty

Medea, blessed (or cursed) with potent magic from the goddess Hecate, was Aeëtes's daughter and a priestess of her father's cult. When she saw Jason, she felt an **instant attachment**, often explained as the work of Eros (Cupid) at Hera's or Aphrodite's command. Medea recognized Jason's decent nature, or perhaps she was guided by prophecy. She offered him magical aid, promising protective charms to accomplish the impossible tasks.

13.9.2 The Bargain

In return for her help, Medea insisted Jason vow to take her with him, away from Colchis, and make her his wife. Desperate, Jason agreed, swearing an oath before the gods. This deal was the pivotal moment: without Medea's sorcery, Jason stood no chance; with it, he could defy Aeëtes. Their alliance, fueled by **love and necessity**, foreshadowed both triumph and tragedy.

13.10 Jason's Triumph: The Dragon-Spawned Warriors

13.10.1 Taming the Fire-Breathing Bulls

Using an ointment crafted by Medea, Jason anointed his body and weapons, granting them temporary invulnerability to fire and bronze. This allowed him to **yoke the monstrous bulls**. Though they spewed flames, Jason endured the heat, harnessing them to the plow. Onlookers, including Aeëtes, were astonished.

13.10.2 The Armed Men from Dragon's Teeth

Next, Jason sowed the dragon's teeth in the furrowed field. Immediately, **armed warriors** sprouted from the soil. Wave upon wave of these Earthborn fighters advanced. But Medea had warned Jason of a trick: by **throwing a large stone** among the warriors, he would make them fight each other. Confused, they turned on themselves, hacking one another to pieces. Jason dispatched any survivors, completing the third challenge.

13.11 Seizing the Fleece and Flight from Colchis

13.11.1 Betrayal and the Sleepless Dragon

Despite Jason's success, Aeëtes planned to kill the Argonauts anyway. Medea, anticipating her father's treachery, guided Jason to the grove where the **Golden Fleece** was guarded by a massive **sleepless dragon**. Some say Medea lulled the dragon to sleep with a potion or a spell. Others say Jason used stealth or cunning. Either way, they took the fleece, hurried back to the Argo, and set sail under the cover of darkness.

13.11.2 Medea's Sacrifice

In some versions, Medea helped slow her father's pursuit by committing a terrible deed: she dismembered her own brother,

Apsyrtus, scattering his remains in the sea so Aeëtes would pause to collect them for burial. This act showed **Medea's fierce loyalty** to Jason—and also her capacity for ruthless action. The Argonauts, unsettled, pressed on, mindful that Aeëtes would never forgive Medea for siding with foreigners.

13.12 The Return Journey: Trials and Losses

13.12.1 Circe's Absolution

Fleeing north and west, the Argonauts eventually reached the island of **Aeaea**, home of the sorceress **Circe** (who was Aeëtes's sister or aunt, depending on the version). Medea sought Circe's ritual purification for the bloodshed of her brother, hoping to appease the gods. Circe performed the rites but banished them swiftly, wanting no part in the feud with Aeëtes.

13.12.2 Past Scylla, Charybdis, and the Sirens

Similar to **Odysseus**'s famed journey, the Argonauts navigated hazards such as **Scylla** (a many-headed monster) and **Charybdis** (a deadly whirlpool). They also encountered the **Sirens**, whose enchanting songs lured sailors to their doom. Here, **Orpheus** proved crucial: he played his lyre so beautifully that it drowned out the Sirens' voices, saving his comrades. Each challenge reaffirmed the Argonauts' unity, blending different talents to survive.

13.12.3 Strange Detours and a Worn Crew

The Argonauts sometimes passed mysterious lands, aided by friendly kings or forced to battle hostile tribes. One story says they even journeyed up the Danube or across the deserts of Libya, carrying the Argo on their shoulders. Over time, the crew's morale wavered, but Jason's leadership held them together. Finally, after months (or years) of wandering, they returned to Iolcus with the Golden Fleece, fulfilling their vow.

13.13 The Fate of Pelias

13.13.1 Medea's Deadly Trick

Triumphant, Jason presented the fleece to Pelias, expecting the throne. But Pelias refused to honor his promise. Outraged, Medea devised a plot: she demonstrated a magic trick where she butchered an old ram, boiled it in a cauldron, and a young lamb jumped out. Pelias's daughters, hoping to rejuvenate their father, followed the instructions but discovered too late that Medea's demonstration had been a **ruse**. Pelias was killed without resurrection, leaving Iolcus in turmoil.

13.13.2 Jason's Banishment

Although Pelias was wicked, the people of Iolcus blamed Jason and Medea for the king's gruesome death. They were **banished** from the city, never to rule. This outcome reveals how an act of vengeance, even against a cruel usurper, can bring condemnation. The couple retreated to Corinth, once again exiles despite having succeeded in the quest's main objective.

13.14 Jason and Medea: The Tragic End

13.14.1 Corinth and New Ambitions

In **Corinth**, Jason and Medea lived for a time, raising children. Jason gained favor with the local king, **Creon**, and eventually sought to strengthen his position by marrying Creon's daughter, **Glauce** (or sometimes called Creusa). This betrayal shattered Medea, who had sacrificed family and homeland for Jason, only to be cast aside in pursuit of political advantage.

13.14.2 Medea's Revenge

Medea exacted a terrible vengeance: she killed Glauce with a poisoned robe and, in her fury, also took the lives of her and Jason's own children to wound Jason beyond measure. This final atrocity destroyed their union, leaving Jason alone and broken. Medea fled, sometimes said to escape in a dragon-drawn chariot provided by her grandfather Helios. The heartbreak and violence of this event underscore how the same brilliance and power that once aided Jason became a destructive force when **love turned to wrath**.

13.15 Jason's Lonely Demise

13.15.1 Loss of Purpose

Without Medea's magic or the trust of any city, Jason's life spiraled downward. He lost his chance to be king, lost his children, and lost the loyalty of his allies. In the simplest accounts, he wandered as a common man, overshadowed by memories of former glory. The man who once led Argonauts across uncharted seas ended as a tragic figure, betrayed by ambition and weighed down by guilt.

13.15.2 A Fittingly Sad End

Legend says that Jason eventually returned to the rotting hulk of the **Argo**, moored at a deserted harbor. While he slept beneath its prow, the ship's prow collapsed, crushing him instantly. Thus, the Argo claimed the life of the hero it once carried, an eerie final note that the grand achievements of youth can become ruinous if neglected or overshadowed by wrongdoing.

13.16 Themes and Lessons

13.16.1 The Power of Teamwork

Jason and the Argonauts highlight how **cooperation** among diverse heroes—fighters, musicians, inventors—can achieve the impossible. Their fellowship reminds us that no single strength is enough. Indeed, a quest of such scale demands many gifts, from Herculean might to Orphic music, from cunning to direct confrontation.

13.16.2 The Consequences of Betrayal

While the Argonauts' voyage succeeded, betrayal defined the final chapters of Jason's story. He turned on Medea for political gain; Medea retaliated with shocking cruelty. The moral resonates strongly in Greek culture: even in triumph, if one dishonors oaths or disregards the sacred ties of marriage and hospitality, **disaster** follows. Jason's downfall underscores the idea that heroism must be balanced by **loyalty** and **honor**.

13.16.3 Mortal Will and Divine Nudges

The gods subtly influenced events—helping Jason cross dangerous waters or igniting Medea's passion. Yet the mortals still bore responsibility for the outcomes. Greek myths often blend **fate** and **free will**, showing that while gods can set up circumstances, humans decide how to act within them. Jason's choices, especially regarding Pelias's death and Medea's abandonment, sealed his fate.

CHAPTER 14

The Underworld

14.1 Introduction: A Realm Beyond Life

In ancient Greek mythology, the **Underworld** (sometimes called Hades's domain) is where souls go after death. Far from a place of simple torment or reward, it is a complex realm with various regions for the virtuous, the wicked, and the ordinary. Ruled by **Hades** and his queen **Persephone**, this shadowy land is neither purely evil nor welcoming. Instead, it reflects the Greeks' view that death is a natural, if sometimes fearsome, extension of life.

This chapter explores the layout of the Underworld, the deities and guardians who preside there, and how living heroes occasionally ventured into this realm. By examining stories of travelers like Orpheus, Theseus, and Hercules, we see that crossing into Hades's kingdom demanded **respect** for strict laws. Mistakes could doom a soul to eternal misery. Through these myths, the Greeks taught caution, reverence, and acceptance of life's final boundary.

14.2 The Geography of the Underworld

14.2.1 The Rivers of Hades

Greek tradition names several **rivers** that define or flow through the Underworld, each representing a key aspect of death:

1. **Styx**: The principal river, whose name means "hate" or "abhorrence." Gods swore unbreakable oaths by Styx, and to cross it was to enter the land of the dead.
2. **Acheron**: The river of sorrow. Many souls were guided across it by Charon's ferry, for a coin placed in their mouths at burial.
3. **Cocytus**: The river of wailing.
4. **Phlegethon**: A river of fire, signifying torment.
5. **Lethe**: The river of forgetfulness. Souls who drank from it lost all memory of their earthly lives.

These rivers gave shape to the Greek afterlife, emphasizing emotional, physical, and spiritual transitions as one left the world of the living.

14.2.2 Charon, the Ferryman

Charon ferries newly deceased souls across the Styx or Acheron (depending on the version). In payment, each soul needed a coin, often placed under the tongue of the dead. Those who lacked this burial rite wandered the banks for a hundred years. This custom influenced actual Greek funerary practices—relatives ensured a coin, or obol, was included with the corpse. Charon's stern demeanor reminds mortals that the journey to the afterlife is transactional and inevitable.

14.3 Hades, Lord of the Dead

14.3.1 A Somber Ruler

Hades (also known as Pluto in some later traditions) is the god who governs the Underworld. While often conflated with the realm itself, he is not evil—just stern, aloof, and impartial. He ensures souls stay in his domain, rarely allowing any to escape. Mortals dread him, not because he is cruel, but because he represents the final boundary none can avoid.

14.3.2 Persephone, Queen of the Underworld

Abducted by Hades from her mother **Demeter**, **Persephone** splits her time between the Underworld and the earth's surface. This duality brings about the **seasons**: her absence causes Demeter's grief and winter, while her return ushers in spring. Persephone's presence in Hades provides a gentler aspect to the otherwise gloomy realm. She takes pity on some souls, or tries to moderate Hades's decisions, though her power is limited by divine law.

14.4 Cerberus and the Gates

14.4.1 The Three-Headed Hound

Cerberus guards the gates of the Underworld, preventing the dead from leaving or unauthorized souls from entering. Depicted with three heads (sometimes more, in older sources), Cerberus represents the savage finality of death. Heroes like Hercules or Orpheus had to confront or calm this beast to achieve their goals.

14.4.2 Judges of the Dead

Beyond Cerberus lie the **Judges: Rhadamanthus, Minos**, and **Aeacus**. These once-mortal kings, renowned for fairness in life, pass judgment on souls, directing them to their proper place. Though Greek belief about afterlife punishments and rewards varies, the idea of moral judgment remains. Wrongdoers might face eternal punishments, while the noble or heroic might receive better fates.

14.5 Regions Within the Underworld

14.5.1 The Fields of Asphodel

Most ordinary souls dwelled in the **Asphodel Fields**, a gray, shadowy expanse where they existed as **shades**, lacking the vigor or passion of life. Neither blissful nor torturous, Asphodel was a place of monotonous existence, reflecting ancient Greek views that the afterlife was mostly a dim echo of one's mortal days, unless one had done something truly heinous or heroic.

14.5.2 Elysium (The Elysian Fields)

Reserved for heroes and the **blessed dead**, **Elysium** (or the Elysian Fields) was a realm of eternal spring, gentle breezes, and joy. Souls here enjoyed feasting, music, and calm. Some traditions say especially virtuous individuals might be reborn multiple times and could attain the **Isles of the Blessed**, an even higher paradise. Though not exactly like modern concepts of "heaven," Elysium was the Greek ideal of rest for the noble or favored by the gods.

14.5.3 Tartarus

The deepest region, **Tartarus**, functioned like a prison for primordial gods and the wickedest criminals. Legendary offenders like **Tantalus** or **Sisyphus** suffered endless punishments for their defiance of divine law. The Titans, once defeated by Zeus, were locked here. Tartarus symbolized a cosmic pit of torment, reinforcing that certain evils demanded **eternal retribution**.

14.6 Famous Visitors: Mortals Who Entered Hades

14.6.1 Orpheus's Desperate Love

Orpheus, a master musician, descended into the Underworld seeking to retrieve his wife, **Eurydice**, who died from a snake bite. His lyre's melodies softened Hades and Persephone, who agreed to let Eurydice follow Orpheus back to life, provided he never look back at her until they reached the upper world. Tragically, at the threshold of daylight, doubt overtook him. He glanced back, causing Eurydice to vanish forever. This story highlights the **fragility of hope** and the absolute nature of the Underworld's laws.

14.6.2 Theseus and Pirithous

Seeking to abduct **Persephone** and wed her, the rash duo of **Theseus** and **Pirithous** ventured into Hades. Outraged, the god trapped them on the **Chair of Forgetfulness**, where they remained in torment. Hercules eventually rescued Theseus, but Pirithous stayed bound. This cautionary tale illustrates the folly of challenging a god's domain out of arrogance.

14.6.3 Hercules's Twelfth Labor

For his final labor, **Hercules** entered Hades to capture **Cerberus**. He used his formidable strength to subdue the hound, with Hades's reluctant permission. This mission confirmed Hercules's might, but also his respect for divine authority. Unlike Theseus or Pirithous, Hercules had a legitimate purpose and left swiftly after fulfilling it.

14.7 Rituals and Beliefs About Death

14.7.1 Proper Burials

Ancient Greeks believed strongly in **proper burial rites**. If a body was left unburied, its soul could not cross into the Underworld and risked eternal wandering. This is why the practice of placing a coin in the mouth for Charon's fare was vital. Even enemies in war might be granted a funeral to ensure harmony with the gods.

14.7.2 Offerings and Sacrifices

To appease Hades and Persephone, mortals offered **black animals** (such as black rams) sacrificed at night. These acts acknowledged the Underworld's power and sought to keep the spirits of the dead from causing harm. Offerings to ancestors were also common, forging a link between the living family and deceased relatives.

14.8 Punishments and Notorious Sinners

14.8.1 Tantalus: Eternal Hunger and Thirst

Famed for hosting a feast where he served his own son to the gods, **Tantalus** was condemned to stand in a pool of water under fruit-laden branches. Whenever he tried to drink, the water receded; whenever he reached for fruit, the branches lifted away. Thus he endured **eternal torment** for his sacrilegious crime. The word "tantalize" in modern usage stems from his name.

14.8.2 Sisyphus: The Endless Boulder

Sisyphus, who tricked gods and defied proper burial, was forced to push a huge boulder up a hill. Each time it neared the top, it rolled back down, forcing him to start over endlessly. This futility represents the **punishment for cunning arrogance**, a lesson on the futility of trying to outsmart death itself.

14.8.3 Ixion and the Flaming Wheel

Ixion attempted to seduce Hera and was punished by Zeus. Bound to a fiery, spinning wheel in the Underworld, Ixion endures constant agony. Like Tantalus and Sisyphus, he epitomizes how certain crimes—especially those against gods—warrant infinite suffering in Tartarus.

14.9 Persephone's Seasonal Return

14.9.1 Demeter's Grief and the Eleusinian Mysteries

Demeter, goddess of the harvest, reacted to **Persephone**'s abduction by letting the earth wither, creating famine. Zeus intervened, negotiating that Persephone spend part of the year with Hades and part with her mother. This cycle explained **seasons**: when Persephone descends, Demeter mourns, bringing autumn and winter; when Persephone returns, Demeter rejoices, bringing spring and summer. The **Eleusinian Mysteries**, sacred rites near Athens, celebrated Persephone's rebirth and promised initiates a hopeful view of the afterlife.

14.9.2 A Lesson on Change and Hope

Persephone's story underscores that even in the gloom of the Underworld, there is a **cyclical hope**. Life reblooms each year, paralleling the idea that sorrow and joy alternate. This concept of cyclical death and rebirth is central to many Greek festivals, bridging the mortal world and the realm of gods and spirits.

14.10 The Underworld in Daily Greek Life

14.10.1 Ghosts and Hauntings

Greeks believed troubled or unburied souls might appear as **ghosts**, causing fear or illness. Some festivals, like the **Anthesteria**, involved offerings to appease wandering spirits, ensuring they returned peacefully to Hades when the festival ended. Such customs highlight the boundary between life and death as both respected and somewhat permeable.

14.10.2 Philosophical Views

Later Greek philosophers, like Plato, used Underworld imagery to discuss the **immortality of the soul** and moral accountability. Plato's "Myth of Er" describes a soul's journey choosing its next life, adding layers of **reincarnation** to earlier beliefs. While not universally adopted, such ideas show the Underworld myth evolving into a moral and philosophical framework about **actions, consequences, and cosmic justice**.

14.11 Heroes Who Emerged Changed

14.11.1 Psychological Transformation

Those who returned from Hades—like Orpheus, though ultimately unsuccessful—were forever changed, carrying **profound knowledge** of mortality. Hercules, after glimpsing the sorrowful dead, completed his labors with renewed empathy. The Underworld experience symbolized a **spiritual test**, teaching humility in the face of divine laws.

14.11.2 Mortality and Memory

By physically crossing the threshold into Hades and back, these heroes confronted the essence of **human mortality**. They learned the fleeting nature of earthly pursuits and the importance of living honorably. Greek myths thus used Underworld journeys to reveal deeper truths: that life's achievements matter, but so do compassion and respect for cosmic boundaries.

14.12 Lessons and Reflections

14.12.1 Facing Death with Reverence

One of the chief morals behind Greek Underworld myths is that **death is a solemn, universal reality**. Even the strongest heroes—Achilles, Ajax, or Odysseus's mother—eventually pass into Hades. Thus, the living must approach death-related rituals and the memory of ancestors with serious respect. Violations, like improper burials, invite wandering spirits or divine anger.

14.12.2 The Impermanence of Achievement

Even mighty kings and heroes roam as mere shades. Material power and earthly pride do not carry over. This message encourages a certain **humility**: life's glories fade, but virtues or crimes may linger in the afterlife's judgments.

14.12.3 Hope in Renewal

Despite the gloom, the Underworld also offers a glimmer of **renewal**. Persephone's springtime return shows that life cycles continue. The Eleusinian Mysteries promised initiates a more comforting afterlife, suggesting that devotion to the gods and moral living might yield a kinder fate than unending grayness. Greek culture balanced these dualities—solemn acceptance of death with the hope that some form of continued essence or reward might exist.

CHAPTER 15

Strange Creatures

15.1 Introduction: A World of Wonders

Greek mythology is known for its vast assortment of **strange and magical creatures**. These beings inhabit every corner of the mythic landscape—from deep seas to lofty mountains, from hidden caves to windswept islands. Many of them present dangerous challenges to heroes, while others serve as guides or companions. Each creature reflects not only the Greeks' imagination but also their attempts to explain natural forces, distant lands, and the mysteries of life.

Whether they are part animal, part human, or wholly fantastic, these strange creatures show the vibrant creativity of ancient storytellers. Often, they convey lessons about **respect for nature** or the price of **hubris**. In some tales, monstrous beasts represent chaos or injustice that heroes must tame. In other tales, a creature's gifts and knowledge can redeem even the darkest moments. This chapter explores a selection of these marvelous beings—from half-horse centaurs to birdlike harpies, from serpentine chimeras to enchanting sirens. We will see how each highlights Greek mythology's blend of **fear**, **wonder**, and **moral reflection** in a world where anything is possible.

15.2 Centaurs: Half-Man, Half-Horse

15.2.1 Origins and Nature

Among the most recognizable Greek creatures are the **centaurs**, beings with the upper body of a human and the lower body of a horse. They are often depicted as wild and unruly, driven by **impulse** and **passion**. Early myths place their homeland in the rugged mountains of **Thessaly**. The most common story of their origin claims they descended from **Ixion**—the man punished by Zeus on a fiery wheel—and a cloud shaped like Hera (named Nephele). This strange parentage underscores their unruly, liminal identity: neither fully human nor fully beast.

Centaurs represent a clash between **reason and animal instinct**. In many stories, they are quick to anger, prone to drunkenness, and lacking in civilized restraint. At feasts or gatherings, a single slight can spark violence. Yet not all centaurs fit this mold; there exists one exceptional figure who defies the norm—**Chiron**, the wise teacher of heroes, known for his kindness and knowledge of arts and medicine.

15.2.2 Chiron: The Noble Exception

Chiron stands apart from his kin. Said to be the son of the Titan Cronus, he inherited a more **enlightened** character. Unlike other centaurs, Chiron dwelt peacefully in caves near Mount Pelion, instructing demigods like **Achilles**, **Jason**, and **Asclepius** in the skills of warfare, music, healing, and ethics. Through Chiron, Greek myths show that even a race labeled as wild can produce wisdom and virtue.

Chiron's ultimate fate came when he was accidentally struck by a poisonous arrow from **Heracles**. Though immortal, he chose to give up his immortality to end his pain, passing his divine privilege to **Prometheus**. This self-sacrifice underscores Chiron's benevolent nature and the respect Greek storytellers had for teachers and mentors.

15.2.3 Conflicts with Heroes

Stories abound of centaurs clashing with Greek heroes. A famous example is the battle with the centaur **Eurytion** at the wedding of **Pirithous**, king of the Lapiths. The centaurs, drunk on wine, tried to abduct the bride and other women. A fierce battle ensued, known as the **Centauromachy**, in which the Lapiths ultimately drove the centaurs from Thessaly. This legend became a symbol of **civilization triumphing over barbaric instincts**.

In art and architecture—particularly on temple friezes—Greeks often depicted the Centauromachy, reflecting pride in reason and law. Still, these portrayals are not purely condemnations of savage centaurs; they also warn of the chaos that erupts when discipline and respect are cast aside.

15.3 Cyclopes: One-Eyed Giants

15.3.1 The First Cyclopes: Blacksmiths of the Gods

The term **Cyclops** (meaning "wheel-eyed") refers to at least two distinct groups of one-eyed beings in Greek myth. The earliest are the primordial Cyclopes, children of **Gaia** (Earth) and **Uranus** (Sky). Skilled blacksmiths, they crafted **Zeus's thunderbolts, Poseidon's trident**, and **Hades's helmet of invisibility** during the Titanomachy. These first Cyclopes possessed extraordinary power and cunning, aligning with the Olympians in overthrowing the Titans.

Far from dull-witted brutes, these primordial Cyclopes embody the **creative force** of forging unstoppable weapons. Once they helped establish Zeus's reign, they remained in volcanic forges, continuing to shape the cosmos through metalwork. Despite their imposing presence, these Cyclopes rarely appear in later myths except as background figures forging divine wonders.

15.3.2 The Younger Cyclopes: Polyphemus and Others

A second, more well-known group of Cyclopes appears in tales of **Odysseus**. The most famous among them is **Polyphemus**, who devours Odysseus's men in the Odyssey. These Cyclopes dwell in remote lands, acting like solitary shepherds. Lacking organized society or agriculture, they reflect a **raw, naturalistic** existence. Polyphemus's brutality is legendary—he imprisons Odysseus's crew in his cave, eating them two at a time.

Yet Polyphemus also experiences heartbreak in later myths, such as falling in love with the nymph **Galatea**, highlighting that even monstrous beings can feel **longing** and **jealousy**. Odysseus's cunning escape from Polyphemus (disguising himself as "Nobody," blinding the Cyclops, and escaping under sheep) remains a hallmark of Greek myth, emphasizing how **intelligence** overcomes brute force.

15.4 Harpies: Wind Spirits of Punishment

15.4.1 Birdlike Females of the Storm

Harpies are often depicted as winged women with sharp talons—part human, part bird. They represent sudden, destructive gusts of wind or storms at sea. In early myths, Harpies could be relatively benign wind spirits, but over time they evolved into malicious creatures that **snatch** food from tables or **carry evildoers** away to be punished. They are especially connected to retribution, functioning like **agents of divine vengeance**.

15.4.2 Tormentors of Phineus

As mentioned in the previous chapter about Jason and the Argonauts, the Harpies' best-known appearance is tormenting the prophet **Phineus**, preventing him from eating. Only when **Zetes** and **Calais** (the winged sons of Boreas) chased them away could Phineus be free. This story shows Harpies as instruments of the gods punishing mortals. However, once that punishment is lifted, they vanish. This balance of cosmic justice resonates throughout Greek myths: punishment must fit the crime, and relief arrives when a worthy hero intervenes.

15.5 Chimera: The Fiery Hybrid

15.5.1 A Terrifying Composite Beast

The **Chimera** stands as a prime example of the bizarre hybrid monsters in Greek myth. Typically described as having the **body of a lion**, a **goat's head** arising from its back, and a **snake for a tail**—with the goat head often breathing fire. This menacing creature terrorized the lands of Lycia, scorching fields and devouring livestock.

15.5.2 Bellerophon's Triumph

The Chimera's story is intrinsically linked to **Bellerophon**, the hero who tamed the winged horse **Pegasus**. With Pegasus's aerial advantage, Bellerophon attacked the Chimera from above. One creative version says he attached a block of lead to his spear, thrust it into the beast's fiery mouth, and the heat melted the lead, suffocating it. By slaying the Chimera, Bellerophon won fame—yet his **hubris** in attempting to fly to Mount Olympus later caused his downfall. The Chimera's defeat thus warns that **even the mightiest monster** can be conquered by strategy, though the hero must remain humble or risk divine displeasure.

15.6 The Sirens: Enchanting Voices

15.6.1 Luring Sailors to Doom

Sirens are often portrayed as part woman, part bird (in later times, part woman, part fish, akin to mermaids), known for their **irresistible singing**. They inhabit rocky islands, using their beautiful voices to mesmerize passing sailors. Once enthralled, the men's ships would crash on the rocks, ending in drowning. The Sirens embodied temptation and the deadly power of illusion, a caution to remain vigilant against **seductive distractions**.

15.6.2 Odysseus's Clever Escape

In the Odyssey, **Odysseus** evaded the Sirens by ordering his crew to plug their ears with wax and by having himself tied to the ship's mast. He alone heard their haunting melody but could not act on the desire to approach. This plan highlighted how harnessing **foresight** can overcome even supernatural allure. Sirens also appear in the Argonauts' journey, where **Orpheus** used his music to drown out their voices, showing that mortal skill can rival enchanting deception when approached with unity and cunning.

15.7 The Sphinx: Riddling Guardian

15.7.1 The Theban Monster

The **Sphinx**, a creature with a woman's head, a lion's body, and eagle's wings (in Greek tradition), famously guarded the city of **Thebes**. She posed a riddle to travelers, killing those who failed to answer correctly. The standard riddle is: "What walks on four legs in the morning, two legs at noon, and three legs in the evening?" The solution—**man**—refers to the stages of human life (crawling as an infant, walking upright in adulthood, and using a cane in old age).

15.7.2 Oedipus's Solution

Oedipus solved the riddle, causing the Sphinx to throw herself from a cliff. His success freed Thebes, leading him to become king. Ironically, solving the Sphinx's puzzle set him on a path toward a tragic destiny of **patricide** and **incest**, showing that escaping one threat does not guarantee overall salvation. The Sphinx's riddle taught a moral about understanding **human nature**—our frailty and progression through life—and how cunning can liberate a city from monstrous oppression.

15.8 Pegasus: The Winged Horse

15.8.1 Birth from Medusa's Blood

Pegasus, though not monstrous, is a magical creature of note. This **winged horse** sprang from the blood of **Medusa** after she was slain by **Perseus**. Often depicted as majestic and pure white, Pegasus flew among the clouds, carrying thunderbolts for Zeus. His presence signaled **inspiration** and **freedom**, connecting the earthly realm to the divine sky.

15.8.2 Aiding Heroes

Pegasus famously aided **Bellerophon** in defeating the Chimera and performed other heroic deeds. Some myths hint that only those with a just or noble cause could ride Pegasus. Bellerophon's ultimate downfall, in attempting to reach Olympus, underscores that Pegasus does not guarantee immunity from **hubris**. Indeed, the winged horse parted ways with him, reflecting that divine gifts remain blessings of the gods, not personal possessions.

15.9 Griffins, Hippocamps, and Other Wonders

15.9.1 Griffins: Lion-Eagles

Griffins, with the head and wings of an eagle and the body of a lion, appear in Greek art and mythology, often as symbols of **guardianship** and **nobility**. They stand watch over gold mines or treasure hordes, representing the union of sky power (eagle) and land power (lion). Though not as central in stories as the Chimera or Sphinx, griffins were a recurring motif in decorative arts, illustrating Greek fascination with combining the strongest traits of multiple beasts.

15.9.2 Hippocamps: Sea-Horse Hybrids

Hippocamps are creatures with the front half of a horse and the tail of a fish, associated with **Poseidon**. They pull Poseidon's chariot across the waves or frolic in underwater realms. While rarely starring in heroic tales, their presence highlights the Greeks' imaginative approach to the sea. They symbolize both the **beauty** and the **mystery** of the ocean, reminding sailors that Poseidon's domain teems with marvelous life.

15.10 Monsters and Morality

15.10.1 Allegories of Inner Conflict

Many of these strange creatures can be read as **allegories** for human struggles. The half-human, half-horse centaur echoes the tension between **rational mind** and **animal impulse**. The all-consuming Hydra might represent unstoppable negativity or corruption, requiring teamwork and cunning to defeat. Thus, Greek myths use monstrous forms to reflect intangible moral or psychological conflicts faced in everyday life.

15.10.2 Hubris and Punishment

A recurring theme is that these creatures arise or remain undefeated when mortals succumb to **hubris**—refusing wise counsel or provoking the gods. Polyphemus, for instance, might never have relentlessly pursued Odysseus had the hero not taunted him with his real name. Similarly, heroes such as Bellerophon or Theseus triumph only as long as they remain respectful of the divine balance. Once arrogance creeps in, the line between hero and monster blurs.

15.11 The Role of the Gods

15.11.1 Creators and Controllers

Some monstrous beings, like the **Nemean Lion** or the **Erymanthian Boar**, come from divine origins or are placed by gods to test mortals. **Hera** released certain beasts to trouble Heracles, ensuring he would struggle for his Labors. Meanwhile, creatures like the Hydra reflect the ongoing tension between **nature's raw force** and heroic duty. The gods either watch from afar or intervene lightly, reminding us that the cosmic order and mortal fates are intertwined.

15.11.2 Transformations

In Greek myths, certain creatures result from **transformation**—punishment or rescue by gods. Arachne, turned into a spider by Athena, or Scylla, once a nymph changed into a monster, show how a single offense or an unfortunate entanglement with deities can twist a mortal into a strange form. These transformations highlight the unpredictability of divine-human encounters.

15.12 Heroes as Monster Slayers

15.12.1 Proving Worth Through Trials

The slaying or subduing of beasts forms a staple in **heroic journeys**. Heracles's Labors revolve around confronting monstrous creatures. Perseus must kill Medusa to protect his mother. Theseus hunts the Minotaur to liberate Athens. Such acts prove the hero's strength and moral resolve. In some ways, Greek myth measures heroic virtue by one's ability to **tame chaos**, whether that chaos is an external monster or an internal flaw.

15.12.2 Compassion or Destruction?

Not all interactions end in slaughter. Jason's safe passage past the Sirens or Orpheus's mesmerizing of the Underworld's guardians demonstrates that sometimes gentler methods—**music**, **wit**, **cooperation**—offer a path to victory. Greek myths thus present a nuanced view: while monstrous threats may require direct combat, intellect or artistry can be equally powerful. The real question is whether mortals maintain **balance and restraint** in the face of primal forces.

15.13 Cultural Impact and Artistic Depictions

15.13.1 Temple Decorations and Pottery

Depictions of these strange creatures abound in **Greek art**—temple pediments, metopes, and amphora paintings. The **Centauromachy** frequently adorned structures like the Parthenon's metopes, symbolizing Athenian ideals of reason conquering chaos. Scenes of Perseus beheading Medusa or Heracles wrestling the Nemean Lion reflect the heroic spirit. Pottery sometimes shows comedic or playful spins on these beasts, reflecting the range of public emotion toward them—from terror to fascination.

15.13.2 Storytelling and Theater

Greek **tragedies** and **comedies** rarely star monstrous creatures as main characters, but references to them pepper dialogues and choral odes. The presence of such references in plays by **Euripides** or **Aristophanes** reveals that these creatures were part of everyday cultural knowledge. Audiences recognized the name "Chimera" or "Hydra" instantly as symbols of challenges or unstoppable menaces. Over time, these images shaped broader Mediterranean art and storytelling traditions, influencing Roman mythology and beyond.

15.14 Philosophical and Moral Interpretations

15.14.1 Monsters as Metaphors

Greek philosophers occasionally used mythical creatures as **metaphors** for personal or political issues. A city overrun by tyranny might be likened to being devoured by a Hydra of corruption. An individual grappling with uncontrolled passion might be said to have the "heart of a centaur." These references reflect how embedded these creatures were in Greek thought—not merely as entertainment, but as vivid analogies for the struggles of mortal life.

15.14.2 Limits of Knowledge

Some monstrous beings, like the Sirens or the Sphinx, represent the dangerous pursuit of **forbidden knowledge**. In answering the Sphinx's riddle, Oedipus escapes immediate peril but later meets his tragic fate. Philosophers might caution that certain mysteries can lead to downfall if approached recklessly. The interplay between curiosity and caution resonates, showing that while knowledge can solve problems, unbridled curiosity can unleash new tragedies.

15.15 Enduring Influence

15.15.1 Legacy in Later Myths

Many of these strange creatures found echoes in Roman adaptations, medieval bestiaries, and modern fantasy literature. The notion of a dangerous, puzzle-posing monster or a half-human, half-beast warrior has never lost its allure. Writers and artists continue reimagining creatures like the chimera or centaur, underscoring their timelessness.

15.15.2 Lessons for Mortals

At their core, these creatures impart lessons on **humility**, **adaptability**, and **moral fortitude**. A monstrous form can test a hero's capacity for empathy—like deciding whether to kill or spare a creature that might have a gentle side. Or it may force the hero to reflect on their own monstrous impulses. Greek mythology uses these encounters to caution that one must face not just external beasts, but also the potential for savagery within themselves.

15.16 Conclusion of Chapter 15

Greek mythology teems with **strange creatures**—each a reflection of deep-seated hopes, fears, and moral dilemmas. From centaurs torn between instinct and reason, to Cyclopes wielding primordial power, to Sirens whose songs tempt mortals off their path, these beings embody a world where **imagination merges with moral inquiry**. Heroes prove themselves by contending with monstrosities that often mirror their own flaws or test their virtues.

Whether through direct confrontation, cunning evasion, or compassionate negotiation, the manner in which mortals handle these creatures shapes their legacy. In all these stories, the line between chaos and order is razor-thin, reminding audiences that courage, respect for the gods, and **self-awareness** remain essential. Strange beings guard the edges of Greek mythic geography—marking boundaries of seas, mountains, or knowledge—and stand ready to challenge any who would cross them unprepared.

CHAPTER 16

Women in Myths

16.1 Introduction: Vital Yet Often Overlooked

Women in Greek mythology occupy a complex space. While gods like **Zeus, Apollo,** and **Poseidon** often take center stage, female figures—from mighty Olympian goddesses like **Hera** and **Athena** to mortal queens and cunning witches—play equally critical roles in shaping myths. They are **mothers, warriors, nurturers, schemers, victims,** and **victors.** Some, like **Penelope,** define loyalty; others, like **Medea,** illustrate how betrayal can unleash destructive rage.

Ancient Greek society was largely **patriarchal,** and this social structure shines through in many myths. Women often lack direct power, yet they frequently drive the narrative's heart—through their intelligence, devotion, or cunning. This chapter explores how women are depicted in myth: from revered goddesses like Athena and Artemis, to mortal heroines or tragic figures like Alcestis and Cassandra, to cunning or magical women like Circe and Medea. We will see how their stories reflect Greek ideals and anxieties, revealing the tension between admiration for women's strengths and fear of their potential to disrupt social order.

16.2 Goddesses: Pillars of the Pantheon

16.2.1 Hera: The Jealous Queen

As the wife of **Zeus**, **Hera** reigns as **Queen of the Gods**, presiding over marriage and childbirth. She embodies **loyalty** to marital bonds but is also infamous for her **jealous vengeance** against Zeus's lovers and illegitimate offspring. Myths often portray Hera plotting punishments or curses, such as the torments inflicted on **Heracles**. Yet she also protects legitimate births and families, signifying her role as a guardian of the **social institution** of marriage.

Hera's contradictory nature highlights how Greek culture both **valued** marriage and **recognized** the tensions within it. Her wrath can be read as a reaction against Zeus's betrayals, giving a voice—albeit harsh—to the emotional fallout of an unfaithful spouse. She thus represents the turbulent power of a slighted wife while still holding divine authority over the household sphere.

16.2.2 Athena: Wisdom and Warfare

Athena (Roman equivalent: Minerva) is the goddess of **wisdom**, **strategic warfare**, and **crafts**. She emerges fully armored from Zeus's head, symbolizing intellectual might and paternal inheritance. Revered as the patron of Athens, she fosters civilization, teaching mortals weaving, pottery, and rational governance.

Unlike other war deities, Athena champions **strategy** over brute force. Heroes like Odysseus or Perseus earn her favor by using wit. She is a **virgin goddess** (parthenos), unattached to any husband or lover, emphasizing her **independence** and focus on city-state well-being. Athena's presence in myths, from guiding Heracles to assisting the Argonauts, reveals a maternal or protective side—but always in the domain of reason and cunning.

16.2.3 Artemis: Virgin Huntress

Artemis, twin sister of Apollo, rules over the **hunt**, the wilderness, and maidenhood. She is fiercely protective of her **purity** and her followers, punishing anyone who violates her boundaries. Stories like that of **Actaeon**—a hunter turned into a stag for spying on Artemis bathing—demonstrate her strict moral code. Meanwhile, she aids childbirth, linking her to the crucial cycle of life.

Artemis's independence and association with untamed nature make her a symbol of **female autonomy**. She stands apart from typical roles of wife or mother, embodying the freedom of the forest. Yet her vengeance can be severe, showing that the goddess's acceptance or wrath often hinges on whether mortals respect her domain and vow to remain chaste if they join her circle.

16.2.4 Aphrodite: Goddess of Love and Desire

Aphrodite personifies **romantic and sexual love**, presiding over beauty and passion. Born from sea foam (in one version) or from

Zeus and Dione (in another), she wields an undeniable power: to stir longing among gods and mortals. Myths show her blessing unions but also causing strife, as in the Judgment of Paris, which sparked the Trojan War.

Though associated with sensual pleasure, Aphrodite can be ruthless with those who deny her domain, punishing them with loveless marriages or impossible infatuations. Her own affairs (like with Ares) highlight the unpredictability of passion. In a patriarchal pantheon, Aphrodite exerts subtle influence, demonstrating that **attraction** can topple even the mightiest.

16.3 Mortal Women of Courage and Caution

16.3.1 Penelope: The Faithful Wife

In Homer's **Odyssey**, **Penelope** becomes an archetype of **marital devotion**. While Odysseus roams the seas for twenty years, Penelope fends off over a hundred suitors pressing her to remarry. She employs cunning—a nightly unweaving of her loom—to delay them. When Odysseus finally returns in disguise, Penelope tests his identity, ensuring no deception. Her loyalty and wit preserve Ithaca's stability.

Penelope's story emphasizes the **virtue** of patience and intellect in a spouse, resonating with Greek ideals of a good wife. She neither challenges social norms openly nor abandons hope. Her steadfastness contrasts with other female figures who cannot endure separation or tragedy. For the Greeks, Penelope is a model of how a mortal woman can be both **clever and devoted**, shaping her own fate within patriarchal bounds.

16.3.2 Alcestis: Ultimate Sacrifice

Alcestis, wife of King Admetus, stands out for her **selfless love**. When Admetus offends Artemis, he faces early death. Apollo arranges a deal: if someone takes Admetus's place in the Underworld, he can live. Alcestis volunteers, going to Hades so her husband might survive. Moved by her devotion, Heracles later wrestles Death to bring Alcestis back.

Her story underscores themes of **conjugal devotion** and **fate**. Alcestis willingly surrenders her life, elevating the concept of spousal duty to a heroic level typically reserved for warriors. Heracles's intervention affirms that such self-sacrifice merits rescue, bridging mortal loyalty and heroic recognition. Alcestis thus embodies an ideal of feminine virtue, lionized by Greek dramatists such as **Euripides**.

16.3.3 Iphigenia and Polyxena: War's Innocent Victims

During the Trojan War narratives, **Iphigenia**, daughter of Agamemnon, is sacrificed to appease Artemis and gain favorable winds for Greek ships. Meanwhile, **Polyxena**, a Trojan princess, is sacrificed on Achilles's tomb after Troy's fall. Both girls are powerless pawns in **political and divine** machinations, symbolizing how women often pay the harshest price for men's conflicts.

These tragedies highlight the Greek acceptance that war's cost extends beyond the battlefield. Iphigenia and Polyxena personify innocence undone by **ancestral curses** or **military ambition**. Despite their passivity, these myths sometimes hint at the deep pathos of families torn apart and the moral complexities that overshadow victory.

16.4 Cunning and Magical Women

16.4.1 Medea: Love Turned to Rage

As explored with Jason, **Medea** is a powerful sorceress, granddaughter of the sun god Helios. Initially, she is a devoted partner who betrays her father to aid Jason's quest for the Golden Fleece. But when Jason abandons her to wed a Corinthian princess, Medea's heartbreak ignites **vengeful fury**—she kills the princess and her own children. This act cements her as one of Greek mythology's most **tragic and terrifying** figures.

Medea's story reflects both the vulnerability and the **agency** of women. She saved Jason repeatedly, but once spurned, she unleashes destruction. Greek audiences saw her as an object of pity (betrayed by an oath-breaking husband) and fear (capable of filicide). This duality underscores the potential for women's repressed power to erupt catastrophically if disrespected.

16.4.2 Circe: The Enchantress of Aeaea

Circe, a daughter of Helios, rules an enchanted island. She lures Odysseus's crew to a feast, then **transforms** them into swine. Yet Odysseus, armed with the herb **moly** (provided by Hermes), resists her magic and compels her to restore his men. Circe then becomes a valuable ally, guiding Odysseus on navigating future perils (Scylla, Charybdis, the Underworld).

Circe illustrates Greek ambivalence toward **female power**. She can be a temptress or a nurturing guide. While initially dangerous, once Odysseus proves his worth, she cooperates. This shift from foe to helper reappears in other myths, indicating that magical women may be integrated into a hero's journey if approached with caution and mutual respect.

16.5 Tragic Figures and Prophets

16.5.1 Cassandra: The Ignored Seer

A Trojan princess, **Cassandra** receives from Apollo the gift of **prophecy**, but when she rejects his advances, he curses her so none will believe her warnings. She foresees Troy's fall, but her predictions go unheeded. Enslaved after the war, she is murdered by Agamemnon's wife, Clytemnestra.

Cassandra's plight—**knowing the future but never believed**—symbolizes the theme of truth overshadowed by disbelief. It also critiques how patriarchy dismisses women's voices. Greek dramatists used Cassandra to highlight the tragedy of clarity unrecognized and the cruelty that befalls those who see destiny but cannot alter it.

16.5.2 Jocasta: Unwitting Incest

In the Theban Cycle, **Jocasta** unknowingly marries her son, Oedipus. When the truth emerges—that she is wife and mother to the same man—she takes her own life. Jocasta's tragedy lies in the **circumstances** of fate. She tries to avoid a prophecy that her child would kill his father, but every effort inadvertently ensures its fulfillment.

Her suffering reflects how Greek myth often punishes even the innocent who attempt to **outmaneuver oracles**. Jocasta, lacking malice, is undone by the unstoppable machinery of prophecy. She thus represents the heartbreak that arises from illusions of control and the powerful inevitability of fate.

16.6 Amazons: Warrior Women

16.6.1 A Society of Female Fighters

Amazons are depicted as a tribe of warrior women living on the fringes of the Greek world, usually near the Black Sea or beyond. They appear in myths fighting heroes like **Heracles**, who must retrieve the girdle of their queen Hippolyta, or Theseus, who battles them in Athens. The Amazons reflect Greek fascination with the idea of a female-dominated society, inverting typical gender roles.

16.6.2 Challenges to Greek Norms

Encounters with Amazons typically end in conflict, as Greek heroes subdue or outwit them. Yet some myths portray partial alliances, as with Hippolyta initially offering her girdle to Heracles. Overall, these stories reveal Greek anxieties about **female autonomy** and the fear of a woman's martial capability. Confrontations with Amazons test whether Greek virtues—discipline, cunning—can tame or outmatch a militaristic matriarchy.

16.7 Goddesses of Fate: The Moirai

16.7.1 Clotho, Lachesis, and Atropos

The **Moirai** (or Fates) are three primordial sisters who **spin**, **measure**, and **cut** the thread of human life. Clotho spins the thread at birth, Lachesis measures its length, and Atropos cuts it at death. Unlike other deities, the Moirai's decisions seem absolute, even over the Olympians. This suggests an underlying cosmic law that outranks personal preference or even divine will.

16.7.2 Symbol of Inescapable Destiny

Their feminine identity underscores an ancient association between **women and birth**. By controlling mortal life from its start to end, the Moirai reflect the unstoppable progression of time. No prayer or sacrifice can sway them once they decree a fate. This concept resonates throughout Greek mythology, where repeated attempts to **cheat prophecy** typically fail. The Fates unify the entire mythic tapestry, guaranteeing each story's ultimate shape.

16.8 Marriage and Power in Myth

16.8.1 Forced Unions

Many myths involve **abductions** or forced marriages—Persephone's abduction by Hades, Europa's by Zeus, or Helen's by Paris. These episodes highlight the vulnerability of women in a society that sees them as objects to be exchanged or seized. Yet, in mythic retellings, these forced unions can lead to significant shifts in power. Persephone's presence in the Underworld changes cosmic rhythms. Helen's abduction ignites the Trojan War, forging legends for generations.

16.8.2 Partnerships of Harmony

Not all unions are forced or tragic. For instance, **Baucis and Philemon** represent an old couple who exemplify hospitality and devotion, receiving blessings from the gods. **Odysseus and Penelope**, though tested by lengthy separation, reaffirm their bond. Such stories demonstrate that Greek myths do celebrate stable marriages grounded in **mutual respect**, even if dramatic tensions overshadow them in more famous narratives.

16.9 Female Solidarity and Rivalries

16.9.1 Allies in Adversity

Women sometimes unite in adversity, forming supportive bonds. The Lemnian women, though overshadowed by tragedy, formed their own society after driving away the men. Medea and Circe, both witches, share familial ties and magical knowledge—though references to their interactions are sparse, they hint at a network of female support.

16.9.2 Rivalries Among Goddesses

Conversely, goddess rivalries show how jealousy or pride can stir conflicts. **Hera**, **Athena**, and **Aphrodite** squabbling over the golden apple of Eris triggered the Trojan War. This event, the Judgment of Paris, reveals how **vanity** and **competition** among powerful female deities can cause devastation on Earth. Such myths do not merely reflect frivolous jealousy but also highlight how powerful female characters can influence world-altering events when at odds.

16.10 Interpretations and Cultural Reflection

16.10.1 Myth vs. Reality

In actual Greek society, women largely lacked political rights and were confined to domestic roles. Myths, however, offer glimpses of female power—divine or cunning. This disparity underscores that while real women faced limitations, mythic narratives recognized the **magnitude** of female influence, though often channeling it into indirect or destructive forms.

16.10.2 Moral and Didactic Functions

Stories like Pandora's opening of the box or Helen's role in the Trojan War can read as cautionary tales about women's perceived "temptations" or blame for certain catastrophes. Simultaneously, examples like Athena or Penelope demonstrate that female wisdom, loyalty, and skill are indispensable. Greek myths thus reflect society's dual sentiment: **admiration for women's virtues** and **anxiety about their potential to disrupt** established order if they step outside sanctioned roles.

16.11 Lasting Influence on Western Traditions

16.11.1 Literary and Artistic Legacies

Greek tales of women—Aphrodite's charms, Medea's fury, or Penelope's fidelity—inspired countless later works. **Roman, Renaissance**, and **modern** authors re-envision these archetypes in plays, poetry, and paintings. Women in Greek myth become universal symbols: the abandoned lover, the wise mother, the vengeful witch, the devout queen.

16.11.2 Feminist Readings

Modern interpretations sometimes cast mythic women as early examples of **resistance** against male-dominated systems. Medea's destructive actions, while brutal, highlight her autonomy and genius stifled by betrayal. Athena's leadership of Athens exemplifies a female model of governance, albeit within paternal frameworks. These readings show how timeless these myths are in prompting discussion about **gender, power, and justice**.

CHAPTER 17

Oracles and Prophecies

17.1 Introduction: The Power of Fate

In ancient Greek belief, **prophecies** and **oracles** shaped destinies both for mortals and gods. From the earliest myths, the power of fate—often revealed through cryptic words—was recognized as unbreakable, even by the mightiest rulers. Kings, heroes, and common folk consulted oracles to learn the will of the gods, seeking guidance for warfare, colonization, or personal crises. Yet, as many stories show, attempting to **escape** or **manipulate** a prophecy often leads one inexorably into fulfilling it.

This chapter examines how prophecy functioned in Greek myth. We will look at the most famous oracular site, **Delphi**, and its priestess, the **Pythia**. We will see how characters like Oedipus, Croesus, and the Trojan princes faced oracles with varying outcomes. And we will explore the moral and philosophical lessons these stories convey—namely, that **divine knowledge** comes at a price, and hubris in the face of fate can bring tragedy. Whether dealing with personal dilemmas or national decisions, Greeks believed that prophecy served as a direct channel from the gods, demanding humility and wise interpretation.

17.2 Oracles in Myth and Society

17.2.1 The Concept of an Oracle

An **oracle** in Greek culture referred both to the sacred site where prophecies were given and to the **divine message** itself. People traveled long distances, bringing offerings and questions. Oracles often spoke in **riddling phrases** that demanded careful interpretation. The premise was that gods, especially Apollo, would answer through a chosen vessel—commonly a priestess or seer—who fell into a trance.

Oracles shaped real historical events: Spartan kings or Athenian statesmen frequently consulted Delphi before wars or major policies. Myths integrated this practice by showing how legendary figures likewise sought divine guidance, weaving oracular pronouncements into epic tales. The synergy between **religion**, **politics**, and **storytelling** made oracles central to the Greek worldview.

17.2.2 Divine vs. Human Insight

In Greek myth, mortals rarely possess direct knowledge of the future. Instead, they rely on oracles to glean partial insights. This dynamic underscores the tension between **human agency** and **divine will**. While mortals might interpret or even ignore oracles, the myths suggest that **fate** eventually triumphs. Oracle stories thus reveal both fear and reverence for cosmic order: mortals can act, but the gods always hold the ultimate vantage.

17.3 Delphi: The Most Famous Oracle

17.3.1 Apollo's Sacred Site

Among all Greek oracles, **Delphi** was the most renowned. Situated on the slopes of Mount Parnassus, it was believed to be the earth's navel (*omphalos*). According to legend, Zeus sent two eagles from opposite ends of the world, and they met at Delphi, marking it as the world's center. Delphi was originally guarded by the serpent **Python** until Apollo slew it, claiming the site and establishing his temple.

Pilgrims flocked to Delphi for centuries, offering tribute to Apollo before posing their questions. The oracle's building complex included treasuries from various city-states, signifying its pan-Hellenic importance. **Delphic maxims**, such as "Know Thyself" and "Nothing in Excess," were inscribed there, reflecting the wisdom associated with Apollo's domain.

17.3.2 The Pythia: Priestess of Apollo

At the heart of the Delphic oracle was the **Pythia**, a woman chosen from the local area. Typically middle-aged, chaste, and from a humble background, she underwent purification rituals, then sat on a tripod over a crevice in the temple floor. Vapors or gasses rising from underground were said to induce a trance-like state. In this altered consciousness, the Pythia spoke Apollo's words, often in **fragmented or cryptic** phrases. Temple priests or prophets nearby would interpret her utterances for petitioners.

Historically, these pronouncements were sometimes recorded in **hexameter** verse. Whether or not the Pythia literally inhaled hallucinogenic gases, her **ecstatic** performance and mysterious answers held immense weight. Myths describing oracular prophecies at Delphi frequently highlight how ambiguous or double-meaning words led to misunderstandings, further underscoring the lesson that mortal hubris or ignorance can twist divine guidance into a self-fulfilling doom.

17.4 Famous Prophetic Stories

17.4.1 The Tragedy of Oedipus

Perhaps the most iconic myth about **unavoidable fate** is the story of **Oedipus**. Warned by an oracle that their child would kill his father and marry his mother, King Laius and Queen Jocasta of Thebes tried to dispose of baby Oedipus. But he survived, raised by adoptive parents in Corinth. Hearing a prophecy that he would kill his father and wed his mother, Oedipus fled Corinth to avoid harming his assumed parents, inadvertently heading straight for Thebes.

Along the way, he killed a stranger (his real father, Laius) and later solved the Sphinx's riddle, winning Thebes's throne and Jocasta's hand. When plague ravaged Thebes, Oedipus sought oracular truth again, only to discover **he** was Laius's murderer and Jocasta's son. This revelation prompted Jocasta's suicide and Oedipus's self-blinding. The moral is stark: attempts to outsmart prophecy often **fulfill** it. Even the greatest intellect cannot outrun the design of fate.

17.4.2 King Croesus Misreads Delphi

A historical-legendary figure, **Croesus**, the wealthy king of Lydia, asked Delphi if he should attack the Persian Empire. The oracle famously replied that if he did, he would **destroy a great empire**. Croesus interpreted this as a green light, only to lose his own empire to Cyrus of Persia. This underscores how oracular statements often hold **double meanings**. Croesus's confidence—bordering on arrogance—led him to misinterpret the prophecy.

In mythic tradition, Croesus's downfall became emblematic of how fortune can reverse swiftly, especially when kings trust ambiguous words without caution. The lesson is to approach oracles with **humility**, seeking clarity and acknowledging one's limited perspective.

17.4.3 Cassandra's Unheeded Warnings

Cassandra, a Trojan princess, gained the gift of prophecy from Apollo, but he cursed her so none would believe her. Her pleas that the Trojan Horse was a trap fell on deaf ears. Her accurate visions about Troy's ruin only heightened the tragedy, as her own family dismissed her as mad. Through Cassandra, Greek myth highlights how prophecy, even if true, is useless if no one heeds it.

Cassandra's fate—enslavement and eventual murder—further shows that bearing knowledge of the future can be more a **burden** than a blessing. The cruelty of her destiny also critiques how societies ignore wise counsel, especially when voiced by a marginalized figure (in this case, a woman overshadowed by male warriors' pride).

17.5 Types of Divination

17.5.1 Direct Prophecy vs. Signs

Not all Greek divination occurred via temple oracles. Some seers or **mantics** read **omens** in nature: flights of birds, animal entrails, thunder. These signs, believed to be messages from the gods, guided everyday decisions—from scheduling battles to choosing farmland. While these lesser omens might lack Delphi's grandeur, they still appear in myths, such as the Trojan War, where each side carefully observed **bird omens** or lightning.

Others, like the seer **Tiresias**, possessed personal gifts of foresight. Transformed into a woman for seven years, Tiresias gained unique insights, valued by gods like Zeus and Hera. His counsel shaped tales like Oedipus's tragedy or Odysseus's journey in the Underworld. The variety of prophecy methods underscores how deeply ingrained the search for **divine guidance** was in Greek culture.

17.5.2 Necromancy and Consulting the Dead

In some myths, heroes seek knowledge from **departed spirits**. Odysseus travels to the Underworld to consult the prophet **Tiresias**, who warns him of Poseidon's wrath and instructs him on how to reach Ithaca. Such necromantic rituals often involved **blood offerings** to draw forth shades. Through these eerie ceremonies, mortals confronted the boundary between life and death, hoping to glean secrets from those beyond. This practice shows yet another dimension of Greek prophecy: the belief that the dead, free of earthly limitations, might hold special knowledge of fate.

17.6 Prophecy's Role in Heroic Quests

17.6.1 Jason's Voyage for the Fleece

In the story of Jason, oracles and signs play crucial roles. King Pelias learned from an oracle to beware a man with one sandal, leading him to challenge Jason with retrieving the **Golden Fleece**. Additionally, the prophet **Phineus** guided the Argonauts past the Clashing Rocks. Here, prophecy both creates the quest's impetus and offers the means to survive. Without oracular input, Jason could not have reached Colchis.

This duality—prophecy creating danger but also providing solutions—appears throughout Greek myth. Oracles test the hero's wisdom in interpreting cryptic instructions, reinforcing the idea that success demands a balance of **divine guidance** and **personal cunning**.

17.6.2 Perseus's Prophesied Patricide

Likewise, **Perseus** was cast to sea with his mother because of a prophecy that he would kill his grandfather, King Acrisius. Trying to thwart this, Acrisius locked Danaë away, ironically ensuring Zeus would visit her and sire Perseus. Ultimately, Perseus accidentally struck Acrisius with a discus, fulfilling the prophecy. Again, no measure of precaution could avert fate's design. Greek mythology repeatedly drives home that prophecies set events in motion, with mortal efforts to dodge them becoming the mechanism by which they come true.

17.7 Philosophical Perspectives on Fate

17.7.1 Early Thinkers on Destiny

As Greek culture evolved, **philosophers** like Heraclitus, Plato, and Aristotle offered varied views on the interplay between fate and free will. While not typically the focus of myth, these ideas influenced how later generations interpreted oracles. Some philosophers maintained that a universal **Logos** or reason governed events, while others emphasized the soul's capacity for virtue or vice.

Though not entirely discarding the notion of prophecy, thinkers like Plato used the concept to explore moral questions: If fate is certain, how do humans remain responsible for their choices? In mythic stories, the tension between inevitability and moral agency remains a central theme. Characters like Oedipus are simultaneously pitied for being trapped by fate and judged for their rash or prideful decisions.

17.7.2 Stoic and Epicurean Views

Later schools, such as the Stoics, believed the cosmos operated on a rational plan, with prophecy reflecting that plan's outlines. Mortals should align themselves with **nature's order**, not fight it. Epicureans were more skeptical of divine intervention, but even they recognized oracles as cultural expressions of **fear and wonder**. Mythic portrayals reflect these debates, sometimes showing acceptance of fate, other times illustrating rebellious struggles.

17.8 Rituals and Consultations

17.8.1 Approaching the Oracle

Those seeking an oracle typically brought gifts—animals for sacrifice, precious offerings—to honor the deity. They performed **purification**—bathing in sacred springs or wearing special garments—believing spiritual cleanliness was vital before receiving divine words. Myths describing oracular visits often mention elaborate processions or the anxious waiting of petitioners. This highlights how oracles were both **religious ceremonies** and community events.

17.8.2 Priestly Mediation

At major shrines like Delphi, a staff of priests managed daily operations. Petitioners posed questions to them, and the priests orchestrated the Pythia's sessions. Myths sometimes show tension between the priests' interpretations and the raw utterances from the oracle. Mortals might suspect that priests used oracles to push **political agendas**. Indeed, some historical accounts claim city-states bribed or manipulated Delphic priests. In mythic contexts, this possibility of corruption or misinterpretation adds another layer to the unpredictability of prophecy.

17.9 The Consequences of Ignoring Oracles

17.9.1 The Trojan War

One reason the Trojan War is so tragic is that multiple oracles warned of the consequences. Hecuba dreamed of giving birth to a flaming torch (Paris) that would destroy Troy. Cassandra repeatedly warned that bringing the Trojan Horse inside the city spelled doom. Yet hubris and disbelief led Troy to ignore these portents. The city's downfall thus exemplifies how ignoring or ridiculing prophecy invites devastation.

17.9.2 Agamemnon's Hubris

Agamemnon, leader of the Greek army at Troy, often disregarded or slighted seers. Before sailing, he ignored a seer's caution about **Artemis**'s anger and ended up sacrificing his daughter Iphigenia to calm the goddess's wrath. After Troy, ignoring warnings about retribution, he returned home triumphantly, only to be murdered by his wife, Clytemnestra. Time and again, Greek myth underscores that disregarding prophecy or seers leads to a violent comeuppance—another caution against mortal arrogance.

17.10 The Legacy of Prophecy in Greek Culture

17.10.1 Lasting Influence

Even after the classical period, Greek oracles and prophecies influenced Roman religion and beyond. The notion of a **destined outcome** guided medieval and Renaissance literature, where tragic heroes often echo Oedipus's struggle against fate. Modern works still reference the Delphic Oracle as a symbol of **mysterious, cryptic authority**.

17.10.2 Connection to Human Psychology

Psychologically, oracles mirror humanity's need for **reassurance** about uncertain futures. Myths reveal a deep-seated fear: that trying to shape or outmaneuver destiny can lead to tragedy. Yet they also provide hope that correct interpretation or wise humility might yield success. The oracular tradition thus unites cosmic inevitability with the **ongoing quest** for meaning, bridging divine knowledge and human aspiration.

CHAPTER 18

Daily Life and Customs

18.1 Introduction: Myth in Everyday Routine

While Greek myths brim with gods, heroes, and epic adventures, they also mirror the **daily lives** of ordinary people in the ancient world. Far from existing in a separate realm, myths influenced how Greeks **dressed, ate, worshiped, married**, and **celebrated**. From small rural villages to bustling city-states like Athens or Corinth, people carried out customs steeped in mythical symbolism. Even humble tasks like baking bread or lighting a household fire could be tied to a **mythic tradition**, paying homage to deities like Demeter or Hestia.

This chapter explores the customs and social structures that shaped everyday experiences in ancient Greece. We will look at family life, education, religious festivals, and how mythic beliefs shaped interactions in the **agora** (marketplace), on the **battlefield**, and in the **home**. By examining these practices, we see how the Greeks integrated **myth and ritual** into routine life, forging a cultural identity that remained cohesive yet diverse across various regions and city-states.

18.2 The Household and Family Structure

18.2.1 The Oikos: Center of Social Life

In ancient Greece, the fundamental unit of society was the **oikos**—a household typically encompassing **nuclear family members**, extended kin, and sometimes slaves. Each oikos was an **economic** and **social** entity, producing or trading goods. The father (pater familias) held legal authority, but mothers played a crucial role in managing the home, raising children, and overseeing day-to-day chores.

Myths reflected the centrality of the household. Goddesses like **Hestia** guarded the hearth, symbolizing communal unity. Heroes often pledged to protect their family's honor or avenge wrongs done to kin. This familial emphasis manifested in real life as strict obligations: sons inherited lands, daughters brought dowries, and religious duties to ancestors structured household rituals.

18.2.2 Marriage Customs and Dowries

Marriages in Greece were often arranged, with **dowries** negotiated between families. Mythic unions—like the forced abductions of Persephone or Helen—mirrored, in exaggerated form, the concept that brides were sometimes "taken" from paternal homes to join their husband's oikos. The wedding ceremony involved feasts, processions, and offerings to gods like Hera (protector of marriage) or Artemis (for the bride's transition from maidenhood).

In daily life, women typically married in their mid-teens, men in their twenties. While love could exist, duty and alliance-building took precedence. Yet myths like Alcyone and Ceyx (transformed into kingfishers after tragedy) or Orpheus and Eurydice (torn apart by death) show how deep emotional bonds were recognized, if often overshadowed by paternal authority.

18.2.3 Children and Education

Children were greatly valued—**sons** guaranteed lineage and property inheritance, **daughters** could form alliances through marriage. Infants underwent a naming ritual on the fifth or seventh day, sometimes referencing family ancestors or revered gods. Mythic parallels include how gods or heroes named children after themselves or ancestors, emphasizing continuity.

Education varied by city-state. In Athens, boys attended schools learning reading, writing, music, and athletics. Girls typically learned domestic skills at home. However, figures like **Artemis** or **Athena** offered female role models of intellect and prowess. While classical myth rarely depicts formal schooling, references to bards (rhapsodes) and moral lessons from epic poetry show that Homeric tales shaped the moral framework of the young.

18.3 Food, Feasting, and Agriculture

18.3.1 Staples of the Greek Diet

Daily meals for the average Greek centered around **grain** (bread, porridge), **wine**, and **olive oil**. Meat was eaten less frequently, usually reserved for **sacrifices** or special occasions. Fish, vegetables, cheese, and fruits supplemented the diet. The goddess **Demeter** (for grain) and **Dionysus** (for wine) were honored for these essential foods.

Wine, diluted with water, was a focal point of **symposia**—drinking parties that combined intellectual conversation with entertainment. Myths about Dionysus highlight the dual nature of wine: it can bring joy or madness, depending on moderation. Agricultural labor—sowing, harvesting, milling—was likewise linked to myths, especially **Demeter's** grief for Persephone, explaining seasonal changes in crop growth.

18.3.2 Sacrifices and Communal Feasts

Religious sacrifices often involved livestock—cattle, sheep, goats—killed in a ritual manner. Certain parts, like thighbones wrapped in fat, were burned for the gods, while the community shared the remaining meat in a **festive meal**. This communal aspect reinforced social bonds and confirmed **piety** toward deities. Mythic narratives of banquets among gods (e.g., feasts on Olympus) parallel these mortal practices, reflecting a cosmic harmony of sharing food.

Additionally, local harvest festivals paid tribute to gods for bountiful produce. In some city-states, processions with grain or wine casks took place, blending **religion** and **celebration**. Myths such as the founding of the Eleusinian Mysteries revolve around agricultural boons, underscoring how feeding the population was both a practical and deeply sacred concern.

18.4 Clothing and Appearance

18.4.1 Common Garments

Men and women wore simple garments like the **chiton** (a linen tunic) and the **himation** (a heavier cloak). These were often pinned or belted, providing comfort in the Mediterranean climate. Footwear varied from sandals to boots, though many worked barefoot. Mythic figures are sometimes depicted in fancier versions, like **Hermes** with winged sandals, or **Athena** in elaborate armor, emphasizing their divine or heroic status.

In everyday life, clothing denoted **status** and **occupation**—wealthy citizens could afford dyed or embroidered fabrics, while peasants used plain cloth. Some myths mention magical clothing or fabric (like the robe that killed Heracles) to show how strongly garments were tied to identity and fate.

18.4.2 Hairstyles and Jewelry

Hairstyles varied by region and status. Men might keep hair short or, in earlier periods, wear it long and braided. Women usually grew their hair long, pinned up in styles that signaled marital status or wealth. Mythic icons like **Medusa** (snakes for hair) or **Aphrodite** (often depicted with flowing locks) reflect the cultural emphasis on hair's symbolic power.

Jewelry—rings, earrings, brooches—was common for those who could afford it. Crafted from gold or silver, these items might bear **symbolic motifs**: Gorgon heads for protection, owls for Athena's wisdom, or imagery of gods to invoke favor. Mythic stories like that of **Harmonia's cursed necklace** illustrate how personal adornment can hold potent significance.

18.5 Religion in Daily Practice

18.5.1 Household Worship

Every home maintained a **hearth** dedicated to **Hestia**, where a small, perpetual flame burned. Family members offered bits of food or wine to the gods at mealtime, believing divine presence kept their household safe. Other domestic altars honored deities such as **Zeus Ktesios** (protector of property) or **Apollo Agyieus** (guardian of doors). Even minor daily tasks, like lighting the fire or kneading dough, could invoke a deity's blessing.

Children learned these rites from parents, ensuring myths about the gods lived on through **oral tradition**. In this manner, mythological narratives—like how Hestia refused to marry and devoted herself to tending the Olympian hearth—reinforced the sanctity of domestic rituals.

18.5.2 Public Temples and Priesthood

Outside the home, each city-state had **public temples** for major gods, funded by communal resources. Priests and priestesses oversaw ceremonies, though most served for limited terms rather than lifelong vocations. Key festivals, such as the **Panathenaic Festival** in Athens for Athena or the **Dionysia** for Dionysus, drew large crowds in processions, athletic contests, and theatrical performances.

In daily city life, worship might involve stopping at shrines, making small offerings at street altars, or participating in a local festival. Myths about how a god founded or favored a particular city (e.g., Athena's gift of the olive tree to Athens) validated these cultic practices, forging a **civic identity** intimately tied to divine favor.

18.6 Festivals and Public Gatherings

18.6.1 The Olympic Games

A pan-Hellenic highlight was the **Olympic Games**, held every four years at Olympia in honor of **Zeus**. Athletes from across Greece competed in **running**, **wrestling**, **chariot racing**, and more, striving for glory and an olive wreath. Myths attributed the Games' origin to heroes like **Heracles** or Pelops, reinforcing the idea that athletic excellence mirrored heroic virtue.

Festival days were akin to holiday periods, with business suspended and truces declared between warring city-states. Victorious athletes became **local heroes**, receiving free meals for life or statues erected in their honor. This tradition extended the mythical focus on **arete** (excellence) into tangible social prestige.

18.6.2 Dionysian Theater

Dionysus, god of wine and ecstasy, presided over major festivals like the **Dionysia** in Athens, where **tragic** and **comic** plays were performed. Citizens gathered to watch new dramas by playwrights like **Sophocles**, **Euripides**, and **Aristophanes**. These plays often reinterpreted mythic stories—Oedipus, Medea, the Trojan War—inviting spectators to reflect on moral and social issues.

While the public spectacle was entertaining, it also functioned as a **civic duty**: the city financed the event, and the audience collectively judged the best plays. This blending of cultural pride and mythic retelling reaffirmed community values, exploring timeless themes of fate, justice, and the divine.

18.7 Work, Trade, and the Agora

18.7.1 The Marketplace

Central to daily life was the **agora**, a public square where merchants sold goods and citizens debated politics. Mythic references adorned statues or building decorations, reminding passersby of heroic ideals. Philosophers like Socrates strolled the agora, discussing virtues that paralleled heroic or civic virtues in mythic lore.

Traders from distant lands brought grain, metals, spices, and luxuries. Greeks prided themselves on maritime commerce, often protected by gods like **Poseidon** or **Hermes**. Myths celebrating voyages—such as the Argonauts—may have inspired real sailors to see themselves as part of a grand tradition of exploration and cunning.

18.7.2 Craftsmen and Artisans

Potters, sculptors, and metalworkers thrived in city-states, producing everything from simple **vases** to ornate temple columns. Scenes from myths—Heracles's labors, Perseus's triumph over Medusa—adorned pottery, turning household items into story-carrying artifacts. Carvers etched gods or mythic beasts into marble reliefs for building façades.

Guilds or artisan families passed down **styles and motifs**. Some sculptors gained renown, like Pheidias, who crafted Zeus's colossal statue at Olympia, a wonder of the ancient world. Myths about Hephaestus, the divine smith, offered a model for craftsmanship, balancing raw skill with artistry, a synergy that resonated in daily production.

18.8 Gender Roles and Social Hierarchies

18.8.1 Men's Sphere

Men engaged in **politics, warfare**, and intellectual pursuits. Male citizens voted in assemblies, served on juries, and might hold public office. Mythic heroes like Achilles or Odysseus shaped ideals of **bravery** and **cunning**, guiding men's sense of honor. The **gymnasium**—a place for physical training—linked athletic prowess to moral virtue, echoing the notion of heroic excellence.

18.8.2 Women's Sphere

Women generally oversaw the **domestic realm**: managing household slaves, raising children, weaving cloth, and budgeting daily resources. Elite women rarely appeared in public, while lower-class women had more freedom out of necessity. Myths about resourceful or tragic women—Penelope, Medea, Antigone—reflected both the constraints they faced and their capacity for **profound influence**. Despite limited civic power, women could shape outcomes behind the scenes.

18.8.3 Slaves and Foreigners

Slavery was common. Many households had **household slaves** who did chores or accompanied children. Large estates might employ agricultural slaves. Myths rarely delve into slaves' perspectives, but some comedic plays humanize them as clever or comedic commentary on social norms. **Foreigners** (metics) could prosper through trade but lacked full citizenship. Their presence in myths is usually minimal, except for tales of exotic lands or the "other," highlighting Greek identity in contrast to foreigners.

18.9 Defense and Warfare

18.9.1 The Hoplite Tradition

City-states fielded armies of **hoplites**—heavily armed infantrymen carrying spears, shields, and wearing bronze armor. Military service was a civic duty for free male citizens. Epic myths like the **Iliad** shaped warrior ideals: valor, loyalty, **kleos** (fame). In practice, warfare was periodic and disciplined, forming a communal identity.

18.9.2 Siege Warfare and Naval Battles

Greek city-states occasionally engaged in **sieges**—like the mythical Trojan War, reflecting prolonged conflict. Naval power was also crucial, especially for maritime cities like Athens. Triremes, sleek warships powered by oarsmen, dominated Aegean waters. Mythic parallels to **Argonauts** or **Odysseus** highlight how voyages and sea battles were part of cultural memory, blending real military technology with legendary sagas of cunning at sea.

18.10 Civic Identity and Mythic Foundation

18.10.1 Founding Legends

Most cities traced their origins to **mythic heroes**. Athens revered **Theseus** as the unifier of Attica. Corinth boasted ties to **Sisyphus**, while Thebes honored **Cadmus**, who sowed dragon's teeth to create its first warriors. Such foundational stories gave civic life a **sacred dimension**, reminding citizens that local governance mirrored ancient heroism.

18.10.2 Festivals and Patron Deities

Each polis celebrated festivals unique to its patron deity—**Poseidon** in Corinth, **Hera** in Argos, **Artemis** in Ephesus. Ritual competitions, music, and dramatic performances reinforced social cohesion. Mythic narratives about these gods, retold each year, renewed communal pride and legitimated political structures. Indeed, monarchy or democracy might be symbolically sanctioned by the city's chosen deity or founder hero.

18.11 Leisure and Entertainment

18.11.1 The Symposium

A hallmark of Greek social life was the **symposium**, an after-dinner drinking party where **wine**, **conversation**, and often recitations of poetry or music entertained guests. Mythic references sprinkled the discussions, as participants compared themselves to heroic or comedic figures. Philosophical dialogues also occurred, with Socrates famously turning symposia into platforms for debate on ethics or love (as portrayed in Plato's *Symposium*).

18.11.2 Theater and Performance

As mentioned, festivals to Dionysus included dramatic contests. Tragedies explored moral dilemmas through mythic plots, such as Aeschylus's *Oresteia* or Sophocles's *Antigone*, dissecting family curses, divine wrath, and civic duty. Comedies by Aristophanes poked fun at politicians and social mores, often using mythic parodies or gods as comedic foils. Theater was integral to daily life, blending **spiritual reflection** with communal entertainment.

18.12 Conclusion of Chapter 18

In ancient Greece, **daily life** was deeply entwined with **mythic traditions**. From the household hearth to the city-state festival, from marriage rites to public debates, the Greeks drew on stories of gods and heroes to shape **values**, **rituals**, and **community bonds**. Men honed their bodies and minds for war or politics, guided by epic exemplars; women safeguarded the household, sometimes echoing Penelope's cleverness or Alcestis's devotion. Meanwhile, oracles and prophecies, feast days, and theater all served as communal intersections where myth and reality converged, reinforcing shared identity.

Though each city-state had unique customs, the overarching presence of epic heritage and divine reverence united them in a broader Greek culture. By weaving mythic references into everyday tasks—lighting a candle to Hestia, naming a child after a revered hero, or painting a vase with Heracles's labors—Greeks constantly reaffirmed their **connection** to the supernatural fabric of the world.

CHAPTER 19

Great Myths About Love

19.1 Introduction: The Power of Love in Greek Myth

Love occupies a special place in Greek mythology, driving some of its most memorable stories. While battles and heroic feats capture attention, many myths hinge on **desire**, **devotion**, or **heartbreak**. Love can spark grand quests, forge unexpected alliances, cause jealousy among gods, or unleash tragic fates. Sometimes it fosters warmth and unity, as in the story of **Philemon and Baucis**; other times, it ends in sorrow, as with **Orpheus and Eurydice**. Always, however, it demonstrates love's **transformative** and **unpredictable** nature.

The Greeks recognized different forms of love—*eros* (romantic desire), *philia* (friendship, loyalty), *storge* (familial affection)—with *eros* being the most potent, often linked to passion or obsession. These myths reflect how the ancients viewed relationships: both **divinely inspired** and **dangerously consuming**. Deities like **Aphrodite** or **Eros** (Cupid) stir hearts, hinting that mortals and gods alike cannot resist love's call, whether gentle or ferocious. This chapter examines key myths that illuminate these themes—tales of longing, sacrifice, jealousy, devotion, and the surprising ways love shapes destinies.

19.2 Eros: The Primordial Force of Desire

19.2.1 Eros as a Deity

Eros (later identified with Roman **Cupid**) is the personification of **romantic love** and **desire**. In some versions of creation myth—particularly Hesiod's *Theogony*—Eros emerges from **Chaos** as a primordial force that drives all beings to procreate and unite. This cosmic Eros is more than a playful god with arrows; he's the fundamental power ensuring that life forms bonds, producing new existence.

Later traditions portray Eros as **Aphrodite's son**, often depicted as a mischievous child or adolescent who shoots arrows to inflame passion. While sometimes gentle, Eros can also be capricious, randomly causing mortals and gods to fall in love, occasionally leading to chaos. These dual images—Eros as cosmic principle and Eros as a prankster—emphasize that love is both **necessary** for life and **dangerously unpredictable**.

19.2.2 The Arrows of Love and Indifference

Myths often mention two kinds of arrows: golden-tipped, which induce **love**, and lead-tipped, which induce **aversion**. Apollo, for instance, was struck by a golden arrow, making him obsessively love the nymph Daphne, while she was pierced by lead, causing her to flee him in horror. Thus, Eros's power is not always benign; it can create **unrequited desire**, heartbreak, and tragedy. This motif underscores how love can be reciprocal or one-sided, shaping countless stories of pursuit and rejection.

Such portrayals show how Greeks used Eros to explain sudden attractions or inexplicable rejections, attributing them to **divine meddling** rather than mere human choice. The moral is clear: no one, not even an immortal, is immune to love's power—yet love's outcomes depend on fortune and timing.

19.3 Orpheus and Eurydice: Love's Devotion and Loss

19.3.1 A Musician's Marriage

One of the most poignant Greek love stories is that of **Orpheus** and **Eurydice**. Orpheus, the greatest musician and poet, could charm animals, trees, and even stones with his lyre. When he married the nymph Eurydice, their joy was brief—soon after the wedding, she was bitten by a snake and died. Consumed by grief, Orpheus refused to accept her loss, deciding to venture into the **Underworld** to reclaim her.

This bold act highlights the **depth of devotion** in Greek myth. Mortals rarely dared to cross Hades's domain, but Orpheus's love and artistic gift emboldened him to try the impossible: returning a soul from death.

19.3.2 Journey to the Underworld

Armed with his lyre, Orpheus descended among the dead, singing so movingly that **Charon** ferried him across the Styx, **Cerberus** let him pass, and the spirits of the Underworld wept at his sorrow. Even **Hades** and **Persephone**—normally unmoved—were touched. They agreed to release Eurydice under one condition: Orpheus must not **look back** at her until both had reached the surface.

This condition tested Orpheus's **faith** and **patience**. The couple ascended the dark tunnels in silence. At the very threshold of daylight, doubt overtook Orpheus—he feared she might not be there, or perhaps he was deceived. He looked back prematurely. In that instant, Eurydice faded away, drawn back into the realm of the dead. Heartbroken, Orpheus lost her forever.

19.3.3 The Lesson of Trust and Impermanence

Orpheus's tragedy underscores Greek beliefs about **transgressing** the natural boundary between life and death. Even the gods' mercy came with strict terms. In failing to trust Hades's promise, Orpheus demonstrated how **human doubt** can doom the most ardent love. Afterward, Orpheus wandered the world, refusing other companionship, eventually meeting a violent end.

His tale resonates as a **caution**: while love can inspire heroic feats, it is also fragile. When fear shatters trust, even the greatest passion cannot survive. Orpheus's story echoes throughout Western culture as a prime example of love's yearning undone by a single, fatal moment of hesitation.

19.4 Eros and Psyche: Trials of Love and Soul

19.4.1 A Mortal's Beauty

Psyche, a mortal princess of extraordinary beauty, attracted worshippers who abandoned Aphrodite's shrines to admire her. Furious at being overshadowed, Aphrodite told her son Eros to make Psyche fall in love with a hideous creature. But upon seeing her radiance, Eros instead **fell in love** with her himself. He whisked Psyche to a hidden palace, visiting her only at night and forbidding her to see his face.

This condition—**no looking** at a beloved's visage—mirrors mythic motifs of love bound by secrecy. The palace provided Psyche with comfort but also curiosity. Her sisters, jealous, sowed doubts in her mind about her invisible lover's true nature.

19.4.2 Betrayal and Separation

One night, Psyche lit a lamp while Eros slept, hoping to glimpse her mysterious husband. The sight of the god of love stunned her, but a drop of hot oil fell, waking Eros. Feeling betrayed, he fled, leaving her alone. Desperate to win him back, Psyche sought out Aphrodite, who imposed **impossible tasks**: sorting a huge pile of seeds, fetching golden wool from dangerous rams, capturing water from a perilous spring, and descending to the Underworld to retrieve a beauty ointment from Persephone.

Each task tested Psyche's **endurance** and **humility**, assisted by sympathetic creatures (ants, a reed, an eagle) or divine hints. Her final challenge—resisting the urge to use Persephone's beauty ointment on herself—proved too great; she opened the box, fell into a deathlike sleep. Moved by her perseverance, Eros revived Psyche with a kiss, and she was granted **immortality** by Zeus. The lovers were reunited on Olympus, with even Aphrodite forgiving the union eventually.

19.4.3 Symbolizing the Soul's Trials

"Psyche" in Greek also means **"soul."** Her union with Eros thus represents the soul's **journey** through trials, guided by love but tested by curiosity, separation, and adversity. In the end, the soul is elevated to divine status, implying that true love, purified by suffering, transcends mortal limits. The myth of Eros and Psyche remains an enduring allegory of how trust, resilience, and unwavering devotion can overcome even divine obstacles.

19.5 Pygmalion and Galatea: Love's Creative Power

19.5.1 The Sculptor's Ideal

In Cyprus, the sculptor **Pygmalion** grew disenchanted with local women, deeming them flawed or unworthy of his affection. Retreating to his art, he carved a statue of a perfect woman from ivory. Each chiseled detail reflected his **ideal** of beauty and virtue. Over time, Pygmalion fell **in love** with his own creation, dressing it, speaking to it, adorning it with flowers, and wishing it were alive.

This reflection on love merges with the concept of **artistic creation**. The Greeks valued craftsmanship—Hephaestus forging wonders for the gods, or Daedalus building labyrinths—so Pygmalion's devotion to his statue signals how an artist might project his **longing** onto a lifeless masterpiece.

19.5.2 Aphrodite's Blessing

During a festival to **Aphrodite**, Pygmalion offered sacrifices, quietly praying for a wife as perfect as his statue. Sensing his sincere passion, Aphrodite blessed the statue with **life**. Returning home, Pygmalion kissed the ivory figure, which grew warm and soft, breathing as a real woman. He named her **Galatea** (in later traditions), and they married.

Their union celebrates love's capacity to **transform** inanimate beauty into living joy, underscoring that genuine desire, coupled with divine grace, can bring about miracles. In broader symbolic terms, the story suggests that the act of creation—whether literal sculpture or metaphorical self-improvement—can be guided by love and lead to profound fulfillment.

19.6 Philemon and Baucis: Love and Hospitality

19.6.1 Humble Couple and Hidden Gods

Amid grand epics, one gentle tale stands out: **Philemon** and **Baucis** were an elderly, impoverished couple living in a small cottage. Unknown to them, **Zeus** and **Hermes** visited their region disguised as travelers. Wealthier neighbors turned the travelers away, but Philemon and Baucis welcomed them warmly, offering the best of their meager food and wine.

As they served, the wine jug never emptied—a sign of divine presence. Realizing their guests were gods, the couple trembled with awe yet continued their **hospitality**. This devotion to the values of **xenia** (guest-friendship) moved Zeus, who determined to spare them from the flood he unleashed on the rest of the inhospitable town.

19.6.2 Eternal Companions

The gods led Philemon and Baucis to a hill, where they watched their region perish under floodwaters. Their humble cottage transformed into a grand temple. Granted a wish, the couple asked only to serve as its priests and to die together. When old age finally claimed them, they turned into intertwined trees at the temple's entrance—forever side by side.

Their love story echoes a gentler aspect of Greek myth: humble virtue rewarded by the gods, true companionship lasting beyond death. Their union stands as a testament to **faithfulness** and **charity**, suggesting that kindness and generosity can transcend mortal frailty.

19.7 Tragic Loves: Apollo and Hyacinthus, Achilles and Patroclus

19.7.1 Apollo and Hyacinthus: Jealous Winds

Love in Greek myth is not limited to heterosexual pairings. **Apollo** loved the handsome Spartan youth **Hyacinthus**, spending days in athletic pursuits. One day, as they practiced discus throwing, a gust of wind (often said to be the jealous wind-god Zephyrus, who also loved Hyacinthus) redirected Apollo's discus, striking Hyacinthus fatally.

Stricken with grief, Apollo refused to let Hades claim the boy. From Hyacinthus's blood, Apollo created the **hyacinth** flower, ensuring his beloved's memory lived on in nature. This sorrowful narrative underscores the **fragility** of happiness, the presence of envy in love, and the possibility of immortality through transformation, a recurring motif in Greek tales.

19.7.2 Achilles and Patroclus: Bonds of War

In the *Iliad*, **Achilles** shares a deep bond with **Patroclus**, so intense that it surpasses mere friendship. While ancient sources debate the nature of their relationship (some portray it as romantic), the emotional tie is undeniable. When Patroclus dons Achilles's armor and is slain by Hector, Achilles is consumed by **rage** and **grief**, returning to battle with unmatched fury, ultimately killing Hector and desecrating his body.

Patroclus's death catalyzes the resolution of Achilles's **anger at Agamemnon** and leads him to confront his own mortality. This episode demonstrates how love can provoke unstoppable wrath when threatened. It also highlights Greek acceptance that emotional closeness between warriors can be as pivotal to a myth's outcome as any divine intervention. Achilles's final sympathy for King Priam, who begs for Hector's body, emerges from his memory of Patroclus, showing love's lingering power to humanize even the fiercest hero.

19.8 Helen and Paris: Beauty as Catalyst for War

19.8.1 The Fairest Woman in the World

The Trojan War, a cornerstone of Greek legend, ignited when **Paris** of Troy abducted (or eloped with) **Helen**, wife of Menelaus of Sparta. Helen's beauty was so famed that suitors from across Greece once vied for her hand, swearing to defend her marriage. That oath turned a private infidelity into a **collective Greek campaign** against Troy.

Helen's role in myth is complex. Some portray her as a passive victim of Aphrodite's promise to Paris, others as a willful participant seeking excitement. Either way, her love affair—born from the Judgment of Paris—steered two nations into a decade-long war, underscoring how **desire** can reshape politics and devastate entire civilizations.

19.8.2 Aftermath and Ambiguity

When Troy fell, opinions varied on whether Helen was truly guilty. Some sources claim she was forced, others that she manipulated events. Ultimately, Menelaus reclaimed her, demonstrating the ancient belief in love's enduring hold, even amid betrayal and death. The Trojan saga underscores how divine whim (Aphrodite awarding Helen to Paris) merges with mortal choices, rendering love a potent yet dangerous force.

19.9 Themes of Sacrifice, Jealousy, and Redemption

19.9.1 Love as Sacrifice

In many Greek love stories, **self-sacrifice** emerges as a key motif. From Alcestis giving her life for Admetus, to Orpheus braving the Underworld for Eurydice, lovers frequently risk or relinquish something dear to save or protect each other. This willingness to **endure trials** resonates with the Greek ethos that devotion demands courage, reminiscent of heroic quests but turned inward toward emotional bonds.

19.9.2 Jealousy Among Mortals and Gods

Jealousy, whether mortal or divine, fuels tragedy. Aphrodite's envy of Psyche spurs epic tasks. Hera's hatred of Zeus's lovers leads to countless torments. Even minor resentments, like Zephyrus's envy over Hyacinthus, cause fatal accidents. Such jealousy underscores how **love's exclusivity** can inflame destructive passions, just as easily among immortals as among humans.

19.9.3 The Potential for Redemption

Yet Greek myths do not always end in despair. Psyche ultimately unites with Eros, Pygmalion gains a living partner, and Baucis with Philemon transcend mortality. These endings reveal an alternate outcome where love fosters **healing** or **divine acceptance**. Even the gods can show mercy when confronted with genuine devotion, suggesting that while love is fraught with pitfalls, it also holds the key to **transcendence** and unity.

19.10 Love in the Broader Mythic Context

19.10.1 Literary Expressions

Poets like **Sappho**, known for her lyric poetry on Lesbos, expressed personal longing and passion, reflecting an intimate take on the epic tradition's grand themes. Though Sappho's fragments are not purely mythic, they demonstrate how love's emotional depth influenced Greek culture beyond hero-centered epics. Tragedians also reworked love stories—Euripides's *Medea* or *Hippolytus*—to examine how **eros** interacts with moral codes and societal constraints.

19.10.2 Philosophical Insights

Philosophers like **Plato** used love myths as allegories for the soul's ascent to higher truth. In the *Symposium*, Plato's characters debate Eros's nature, citing mythic references (e.g., Aristophanes's story of humans split in half seeking their other half). This philosophical extension of mythic love focuses on how desire can prompt individuals to **pursue beauty and wisdom**, bridging physical attraction with spiritual ideals.

Hence, Greek mythic love influences multiple spheres: everyday worship of Eros or Aphrodite, poetic tradition, and philosophical discourse on how love might elevate or enslave the human spirit.

CHAPTER 20

The End of an Age

20.1 Introduction: From Mythic Splendor to Changing Tides

This final chapter addresses the **twilight** of the classical mythological world. Although Greek myths continue to fascinate, the actual cultural and religious landscape in which they thrived eventually shifted. Over centuries, new philosophies, political upheavals, and outside influences reconfigured Greek identity. The **Olympian gods** did not vanish overnight, but the society that worshipped them with unwavering devotion evolved—encountering **Hellenistic** expansions, Roman dominion, and eventually **Christian** influence.

In this concluding section, we will see how Greek mythic tradition **transformed** under these changes. The heroes' age gave way to historical conquests—Alexander the Great's campaigns, the absorption into the Roman Empire—and philosophical movements that questioned literal belief in gods. We examine the final glimpses of an era when Zeus's thunder and Athena's guidance shaped mortal destiny and how their stories were adapted, allegorized, or merged into broader cultural tapestries. This "end of an age" highlights how myths remain alive in new contexts, even as their original religious framework fades.

20.2 The Trojan War as the Last Great Epic

20.2.1 A Climax of the Heroic Era

Greek storytellers often cast the **Trojan War** as a culminating point—the final massive conflict involving demigods and direct divine intervention. Many heroes died at Troy or shortly after returning home, and some traditions said that with the war's end, the **Age of Heroes** closed. This sense of finality arises in works like Homer's *Iliad*, which, though focusing on Achilles's wrath, implies an entire civilization's pinnacle of martial prowess.

Myths following the war frequently describe chaotic aftermaths (Odysseus's protracted journey, Agamemnon's murder) or partial attempts to rebuild (like Aeneas's flight, leading to Rome's mythic founding). The Trojan War thus stands as a **literary boundary**, marking the transition from shining heroics to mortal fragility, and setting the stage for new forms of governance and culture.

20.2.2 Diminishing Divine Presence

During and after Troy's fall, gods like **Poseidon**, **Athena**, or **Apollo** meddled but also suffered personal affronts or lost mortal followers. Greek dramas depict a sense that the **gods withdrew** somewhat, letting mortal fates unwind. Such stories reflect an evolving worldview where direct theophanies (divine appearances) became less common, possibly as rationalist thought gained ground in city-states. The heroic age ended not just because the heroes perished, but because the gods' **active guidance** waned.

20.3 Fate of the Olympians in the Hellenistic World

20.3.1 Alexander the Great and Syncretism

With the rise of **Alexander the Great** in the 4th century BCE, Greek influence spread from Egypt to India, blending with local cultures. Alexander, claiming descent from **Heracles** or **Achilles**, invoked mythic lineage to legitimize his rule. He founded cities named **Alexandria**, establishing Greek-style temples and adopting foreign gods into his pantheon. This cultural **syncretism** meant that Greek gods merged with or were identified as equivalents to Egyptian, Persian, or other regional deities (e.g., Zeus-Ammon in Egypt).

In effect, the Olympians gained new names and guises, reflecting the elasticity of mythic tradition. Temples dedicated to "Zeus-Ammon" highlight how Greek theology adapted to foreign beliefs. The core identity of the Olympians remained, but their worshippers recognized that gods might appear differently elsewhere. This broad perspective still valued Greek myths but placed them in a **cosmopolitan** context.

20.3.2 Philosophical Outlooks on the Gods

By the Hellenistic period, thinkers like the **Stoics** or **Epicureans** offered new frameworks. **Stoics** saw Zeus as a cosmic mind, identifying mythology as allegory for nature's rational order. **Epicureans** minimized divine interference, viewing gods as distant or uninterested. Myths persisted as moral stories or poetic traditions but were no longer taken as literal truths by many educated elites.

Despite these changing interpretations, popular festivals and devotions continued at local shrines. The city-state religion remained deeply woven into civic life, but an intellectual shift was underway. Myths were revered for their **aesthetic** and **traditional** value, not necessarily for describing actual events. This gradual reevaluation foreshadowed the transformations soon to come.

20.4 Roman Domination and Adaptation

20.4.1 Rome's Adoption of Greek Myths

As Rome expanded into Greece (2nd century BCE onward), Greek culture heavily influenced Roman religion, literature, and art. The Romans identified Greek gods with their own: **Zeus** with **Jupiter**, **Hera** with **Juno**, **Ares** with **Mars**, etc. The poet **Virgil**, in the *Aeneid*, drew on Trojan War myths—Aeneas fleeing Troy to found Rome. This myth effectively **linked** Roman identity to the Greek heroic age, placing Rome as the inheritor of Trojan (and thus Greek) destiny.

Roman authors like Ovid in his *Metamorphoses* reworked Greek stories, emphasizing transformations and moral lessons. The Olympians thus lived on in Roman culture, albeit under Latinized names and adapted moral contexts. This stage sustained Greek myth's survival, guaranteeing that even as Greek poleis declined politically, their mythic heritage thrived in the Roman mainstream.

20.4.2 Shrinking Hellenic Independence

Politically, many Greek city-states lost autonomy, paying tribute to or being directly ruled by Rome. Traditional festivals continued, but the **empire's** official recognition of certain cults overshadowed local practices. Over time, philosophical schools in Rome—like the later **Neoplatonists**—merged Greek theological concepts with Roman state religion, creating a vast syncretic environment.

Though the worship of Olympians persisted in various corners, it faced competition from Eastern mystery cults (e.g., Isis, Mithras) and eventually from Christianity. By the imperial era, the old Greek religion was merely one thread in a vast tapestry of Roman paganism.

20.5 Emergence of Christianity and Decline of Paganism

20.5.1 Early Christian Encounters

From the 1st century CE onward, **Christianity** spread across the Mediterranean. Early Christians denounced **pagan** gods as false or demonic, often condemning worship of Zeus or Apollo. Over centuries, as Christianity gained imperial support—particularly after Emperor Constantine in the 4th century CE—the empire gradually shifted from official tolerance of multiple cults to a **predominantly Christian** identity.

For the Greek pantheon, this meant diminishing state patronage, fewer new temples, and eventual bans on sacrifices. Philosophical schools that revered Olympians or taught them as cosmic allegories struggled under Christian emperors. The famed Temple of Delphi, once a powerhouse, lost relevance as Christian bishops rose in influence, culminating in Emperor Theodosius I forbidding pagan rites by the late 4th century CE.

20.5.2 Transformation into Cultural Lore

Even as official worship of the Olympians faded, Greek myths did not vanish. They survived in literature, learned commentaries, and popular storytelling. By the early medieval period, many in the Greek-speaking world recognized the gods as **mythic or allegorical** rather than literal. Christian theologians like Clement of Alexandria or Eusebius sometimes cited Greek myths to illustrate moral or immoral behaviors, turning them into **didactic** examples rather than religious truths.

Thus, the Olympians and hero tales passed from living religion to **cultural heritage**, studied for their poetic or philosophical worth rather than as objects of devotion. Monks copied manuscripts of Homer or Hesiod, preserving them ironically in a Christian context. This shift from devout worship to classical learning marked a definitive end to the age where Greek myth formed the spiritual backbone of a people.

20.6 Last Echoes: The Neoplatonists and Hermetic Traditions

20.6.1 Philosophical Revival

Some pockets of late antiquity, like certain **Neoplatonist** circles in Athens or Alexandria, clung to a **revived** pagan spirituality. Philosophers like **Proclus** or **Iamblichus** practiced theurgy (rituals invoking gods), seeing them as emanations of the One or the Divine Mind. They reinterpreted myths as **esoteric allegories** about the soul's ascent.

While this movement was rich in intellectual depth, imperial and public support had mostly shifted Christian, leading to the closure of philosophical schools. By the 6th century, Emperor Justinian suppressed the Academy in Athens, symbolically ending the last major pagan stronghold. The Olympians thus lingered in small philosophical enclaves but not as a widespread religious force.

20.6.2 Hermetic and Occult Circles

A few occult traditions, drawing on **Hermes Trismegistus** or Orphic rites, carried remnants of Greek myth and ritual into clandestine societies. They identified gods with cosmic principles or hidden planetary powers. Though never mainstream, these groups influenced medieval and Renaissance esotericism in Europe, ensuring Greek mythic elements survived in **astrology, alchemy**, and **magical** texts.

Hence, even beyond official worship, Greek myths found new expressions, bridging cultures and eras through symbolic reinterpretations. The "end of an age" was less a total extinction than a metamorphosis from shared public piety to specialized, often secret, knowledge.

20.7 Cultural and Artistic Legacy

20.7.1 The Renaissance Revival

Greek mythology reemerged prominently in the **Renaissance**, when European scholars rediscovered classical texts. Artists like **Botticelli** or **Titian** painted mythic scenes—Venus rising from the sea, Diana hunting in moonlit forests—infusing them with Christian or humanist allegories. Writers like Shakespeare drew on Ovid's metamorphoses, referencing Greek stories for universal themes of love and transformation.

This revival showed that, although Greek religion had ended as a living faith, the **mythic narratives** retained universal resonance, bridging ancient wisdom and new creative impulses. Gods like Zeus or Hermes became **literary** figures, their images frequently displayed in architectural friezes or palace frescoes.

20.7.2 Modern Interpretations

In modern times, Greek myths continue to inspire literature, film, art, and psychoanalytic theory (Carl Jung, for instance, referenced Greek archetypes). Writers reimagine characters like Medea or Oedipus for contemporary audiences, exploring timeless dilemmas of love, fate, ambition, and guilt. The shift from worship to **symbolic storytelling** ensures these myths remain potent, reflecting the human condition's constants: longing for meaning, grappling with destiny, and searching for moral insight.

20.8 Philosophical and Historical Reflections

20.8.1 Humanizing the Gods

Over time, Greek myths gradually **humanized** the gods—downplaying cosmic might in favor of moral lessons. Philosophers like Xenophanes critiqued anthropomorphic deities, prompting intellectual circles to view myths as **metaphors** for ethics or cosmic phenomena. This perspective, deepening across centuries, laid groundwork for allegorical interpretations that overshadowed literal worship.

20.8.2 Questioning the Past

Greek historians—Herodotus, Thucydides—already questioned purely mythic accounts of war or founding events, seeking rational explanations. By the Roman era, readers saw **mythic genealogies** or monstrous creatures as either poetical exaggerations or symbolic parables. The Trojan War, once an absolute marker of heroic reality, was approached with skepticism or romantic nostalgia.

Such critical stances mirrored broader cultural maturity: a society might revere its mythic past but also strive for historical clarity. This contributed to the decline of naive acceptance of myths, while preserving them as **cultural cornerstones** of identity.

20.9 The Enduring Spirit of Greek Myth

20.9.1 A Living Legacy

Even though the direct worship of Zeus, Athena, and other Olympians ceased, the **stories** lived on robustly. Medieval Byzantine traditions, Renaissance humanism, Enlightenment scholarship, and modern popular culture keep reinterpreting Greek myths. They appear in everything from psychological models (the Oedipus complex) to modern fantasy literature. Across centuries, these narratives remain a **touchstone** for exploring archetypal conflicts—fate vs. free will, mortals vs. gods, passion vs. reason.

20.9.2 Eternal Appeal

Why do these myths persist? They address fundamental human experiences—love and jealousy, courage and betrayal, the quest for glory, the acceptance of mortality. Each generation finds fresh meaning in Icarus's fall, Prometheus's defiance, or Persephone's cyclical journey. The "end of an age" for ancient Greek religion did not end the myths' power to reflect and shape human thought. Instead, they continue in new forms, bridging the ancient and the modern.

20.10 Conclusion of Chapter 20

The **end of an age** in Greek mythology meant the gradual fading of the Olympians' living cults under the pressures of **philosophical change**, **Hellenistic syncretism**, **Roman governance**, and, ultimately, the **rise of Christianity**. Temples fell silent or repurposed, oracles closed, and direct worship gave way to allegory and literature. Yet the **myths themselves**—once core religious narratives—survived and thrived, reborn as cultural, artistic, and intellectual treasures.

Their survival underscores that myths do not die with the civilizations that birthed them. Instead, they transform, carrying ancient truths into new epochs. As we conclude this comprehensive journey through Greek mythology—from cosmic creation to the dimming of the gods—one truth remains evident: these stories still **captivate**, spurring imagination and reflecting humanity's deepest hopes, fears, and moral inquiries. We close with the knowledge that Greek myth, though no longer a living faith, endures as a **legacy** of creativity, moral reflection, and timeless fascination—an eternal testament to the power of storytelling and the enduring questions of existence.

Help Us Share Your Thoughts!

Dear reader,

Thank you for spending your time with this book. We hope it brought you enjoyment and a few new ideas to think about. If there was anything that didn't work for you, or if you have suggestions on how we can improve, please let us know at **kontakt@skriuwer.com**. Your feedback means a lot to us and helps us make our books even better.

If you enjoyed this book, we would be very grateful if you left a review on the site where you purchased it. Your review not only helps other readers find our books, but also encourages us to keep creating more stories and materials that you'll love.

By choosing Skriuwer, you're also supporting **Frisian**—a minority language mainly spoken in the northern Netherlands. Although **Frisian** has a rich history, the number of speakers is shrinking, and it's at risk of dying out. Your purchase helps fund resources to preserve and promote this language, such as educational programs and learning tools. If you'd like to learn more about Frisian or even start learning it yourself, please visit **www.learnfrisian.com**.

Thank you for being part of our community. We look forward to sharing more books with you in the future.

Warm regards,
The Skriuwer Team